A COMPARATIVE STUDY OF REGIONAL AUTONOMY MODELS IN JAMMU AND KASHMIR

A COMPARATIVE STUDY OF REGIONAL AUTONOMY MODELS IN JAMMU AND KASHMIR

Dr Showkat Ahmad

KALPAZ

First Published, 2018

Published by

Kalpaz Publications
C-30, Satyawati Nagar,
Delhi – 110052
E-mail: kalpaz@hotmail.com
Ph.: 9212142040

Printed at: G. Print Process, Delhi

Cataloging in Publication Data—DK
Courtesy: D.K. Agencies (P) Ltd. <docinfo@dkagencies.com>

Ahmad, Showkat, author.
A comparative study of regional autonomy models in Jammu and Kashmir / Dr Showkat Ahmad.
pages cm
Includes bibliographical references and index.
ISBN 9789386397171 (HB)

1. Regionalism—India—Jammu and Kashmir. 2. Local government—India—Jammu and Kashmir. 3. Ethnicity—India—Jammu and Kashmir. 4. Decentralization in government—India—Jammu and Kashmir. 5. Jammu and Kashmir (India)—Politics and government. I. Title.

LCC JQ620.K32A36 2018 | DDC 320.809546 23

Contents

Preface

The book offers an understanding of the major debates surrounding the core concepts and complexities in the contemporary Kashmir politics. The State of Jammu and Kashmir consists of three main cultural units and geographical divisions, namely- Jammu, Kashmir and Ladakh. It came into existence as a result of the conquest of Punjab by the British in 1845. The territories of Jammu and Kashmir which formed a part of the Sikh state were separated from it. The province of Kashmir and Gilgit were handed over to Gulab Singh, a feudatory of the Sikhs, for a Cash payment of Seventy-five Lakh Rupees by the British. As a result, Gulab Singh was recognised as the Maharaja of Jammu and Kashmir and he laid the foundation of Dogra rule in the state. The Dogras retained the feudal structure of society which the earlier rulers had already established in the state. The Muslim Subjects who formed bulk of the population bore heaviest brunt and burden of the Dogra autocracy which was restrictive, region centric, despotic and exploitative. The freedom movement during 1930's in Jammu and Kashmir was actually a vigorous struggle against the oppressive rule of the Dogras.

The state of Jammu and Kashmir has many peculiar features and problems of its own. It has figured prominently as a factor, symbolic of the partition both in terms of tension within its socio-political fabric and hostilities in the subcontinent. Its geo-political features, cultural heterogeneity, social and economic contradictions bred during a century of despotic rule under British hegemony and accentuated by the circumstances of partition and the dialects of the country have all added to the complexity of the problem.

The problem in Jammu and Kashmir has often been described with two dimensions: internal and external. The present work analyses Kashmir problem in three dimensions, External, Federal and Internal. External dimension involves the engagement between New Delhi and

Islamabad. The Federal dimension, which is often described as internal dimension as situation actually prevailing within Jammu and Kashmir is grossly ignored. It is about the spirit of the instrument of accession, Autonomous Status of the state of Jammu and Kashmir, provisions of the Article 370 of the Constitution of India, Delhi Agreement of 1952 and Indira-Sheikh Agreement of 1975. The third and the most critical and continuously ignored aspect of the conflict in Jammu and Kashmir is its internal dimension (between the regions within Jammu and Kashmir). In fact, the people are continuously in conflict among themselves within the state. Therefore, it would be no exaggeration to say that regional conflict within Jammu and Kashmir is more rigorous than the level of conflict between state and the Centre even the State of Jammu and Kashmir would be granted Greater Autonomy or Regional Autonomy as advocated by the largest political parties of the state such as National Conference or Self Rule as demanded by Peoples Democratic Party or as Regional autonomy proposal advocated by Balraj Puri etc. The conflict will not end rather, setting the power for conflict between New Delhi and Kashmir will bring to the fore underlying conflicts among the regions and sub-regions.

The deeply plural character of the Jammu and Kashmir politics makes it imperative to devise instruments and processes for restructuring the rules of the game so as to ensure that power sharing is inclusive. This is necessary not only for reasons of equality and legitimacy but also to 'make it work' in the long term. To judge by the historical record, no movement in the state has succeeded in achieving its objectives unless it was inclusive in its political character and social base and unless it represented the political interests of all the groups, as distinct from those in the majority. This explains the failure of the Kashmiris secessionist agenda in the 1950's as well as the 1990's. They demanded the right to self-determination in the name of "the people of Jammu and Kashmir" but campaigned on behalf of only the majority community; Kashmiri Muslims. The minority social groups, in fact, sought autonomy from the Kashmir Valley. The collective and consistent opposition of the state`s linguistic, regional and religious minorities checkmated the Kashmiri Muslims demand for secession. Likewise, the most important reason for the failure of Jammu`s political demands, ranging from regional political autonomy and a regional council to separate state- has been the lack of mass support in the region. The Ladakhi Buddhist's have not succeeded in securing Union Territory Status for Ladakh because the idea is bitterly opposed by the Kargil Muslims, who make up nearly half of Ladakh's population. The alternative political goal of an Autonomous Hill Council was achieved only after they persuaded Ladakhi Muslims to support their Demand. The story of the Kashmiri Pundits is no different. This shows that Kashmir's Self Rule or Autonomy from New Delhi will be acceptable to different cross-sections of society only if it is viewed as point of a broader process of devolving power to regions.

The conflict at the Sub-regional level is also too sharp cutting across the political and ideological differences; there is a strong movement in Doda District for the creation of Chenab Valley Autonomous Hill Development Council. The twin frontier districts of Rajouri and Poonch too have been campaigning for separate Development Council as the fruits of infrastructure and industrial development are concentrated around the capital cities of Jammu and Srinagar alone. However, if three distinct regions of the Jammu and Kashmir state - Jammu, Kashmir and Ladakh do not find common ground with each other, the conflict can never find a resolution.

The present work is divided into five chapters that explore the different dimensions of the regional problem within the State of Jammu and Kashmir. The first chapter introduces the subject of the study. It defines the problem and its different aspects with focus on the historical background of the state of Jammu and Kashmir. It attempts at highlighting the regional rift among the different regions of the state before 1947.

The second chapter analyses the identity and regional aspirations within the state of Jammu and Kashmir since 1947. The nature of these regional tensions has been dealt extensively. The focus of study in this chapter is how these regions are divergent with their issues of development, ideology and representation. The study also focuses on the problems of sub-regional identities within Jammu and Kashmir.

The third chapter discusses the different Regional Autonomy Models in Jammu and Kashmir. These include: National Conference's Regional Autonomy Model, Balraj Puri's Regional Autonomy Model, Peoples Democratic Party's Self-Rule Document, Ladakh Autonomous Hill Development Council Model and Chenab Formula Model. These formulas or models have been dealt extensively.

The fourth chapter critically analyses these Regional Autonomy Models, proposed from time to time, to overcome the regional problems within and without.

The fifth chapter ends up with Summary and Conclusions.

Writing this work has proven to be rewarding experience than I have envisioned. The journey has been intellectually rewarding. The present author takes full responsibility for any errors, omissions or criticism.

I hope that the book is timely and provides an insightful discourse into the changing dynamics of Kashmir Politics in the light of the contemporary times and circumstances. I hope this little effort will be worthwhile and my purpose fulfilled if the readers find it useful. Any suggestions for further improvement are welcome.

Acknowledgement

It is my privilege to express my profound sense of gratitude to my esteemed supervisor and teacher Professor Ravinderjit Kaur whose keen interest, able guidance and insistence on better quality of work inspired me to work hard. It is her open mindedness, objective way of thinking and deep understanding in research that able me to collect relevant data, interpret and analyse it in a proper way. I am also indebted to her for supervising this work with critical evaluation and high dedication.

I feel honoured to extend my special thanks to my respected teachers of the Department of Political Science, University of Kashmir for their valuable suggestions and whole-hearted cooperation. I am also thankful to them for their insistence to publish this work.

I am also thankful to the Non-Teaching Staff of the Department Library and Alama Iqbal Library, University of Kashmir for their constant support and assistance and helping me for providing relevant data for the completion of this work. Special thanks also go to the University of Kashmir for proving me an opportunity for the completion of this work.

No words would be sufficient to express my gratitude to all my colleagues and friends for their valuable suggestions and encouragement throughout this work.

I want to thank my esteemed parents for all their efforts and challenge that they have faced for bringing me where I stand today. I am extended sincere thanks for their encouragement, love, affection and constant emotional support for the completion of this work.

Lastly, I am very much thankful to the Kalpaz Publications, New Delhi for insisting me to publish this work and providing me thoughtful suggestions from time to time for the same.

Dr Showkat Ahmad

Chapter - 1

Introduction

Jammu and Kashmir State came into being as a single political and geographical entity following the treaty of Amritsar between the British Government and Gulab Singh signed on March 16, 1846. This treaty made Gulab Singh agreed to pay (75,00,000) seventy-five lakh Rupees (Nanaksahi) towards British East India Company. With the assistance of the force by the East India Company, Gulab Singh was in the position to get the province of Kashmir on November 9, 1846.[1]

In fact, the state under the Dogra rule was not an independent state in real sense. There were limitations put upon the state sovereignty in its external affairs. Article 10 of the treaty of Amritsar made it clear that Maharaja Gulab Singh had accepted the supremacy of the British Government. With the title of "Maharaja" Gulab Singh imposed himself over the people of the state and the majority of the population of the state was ruthlessly oppressed.[2] After a short period of time, the British Government started interfering into the internal matters of the state. On the complaints submitted to the British Government regarding the oppression by the Dogra rulers, Rtd. R.G. Taylor was sent to verify these complaints. In his letter to Gulab Singh, dated 29th November 1847, Lawrence warned Maharaja as "the British Government will not permit tyranny in 'Cashmere' and the country under your rule, and that if you will not check yourself, some other engagement will be made for the protection of the hilly people".[3] It was the rule of one man with all powers – legislative, judicial, executive in one hand, and the same was responsible for tyranny over people of Kashmir on the other. To run the administrative affairs, the state was divided into regions and sub-regions. Each division was sub-divided into districts headed by district officers.[4] So far as the Kashmir division is concerned it was divided into two major divisions, Kamraz and Maraz. Jammu province had four districts, the frontier was divided into two districts, Ladakh was put under a local government and Gilgit was put under the control of commanding officer of the state.[5]

Since Gulab Singh remained largely pre-occupied with suppressing the voices of dissent within the state, therefore he could not build a proper administrative system. Hence, it was in the time of Ranbir Singh who succeeded the Maharaja that concrete steps were taken regarding the consolidation of the state.[6] In order to improve the administration, Ranbir Singh studied the position of the state thoroughly and found that main cause of haphazardness was that the provinces of Jammu and Kashmir were so big that large areas remained practically un-administered. First step towards this end was that the provincial administration was modified and the provinces were redistributed in districts, administered by district officers.[7] The Jammu province was divided into seven Wazarats; Jammu Khas, Jasrota, Ram Nagar, Reasi, Udhampur, Nowshera Khas and Minawar. Similarly, the Kashmir province was divided into six Wazarats; Shahar-i-Khas, Anantnag, Shopian, Pattan, Kamraj and Muzaffarabad. The only difference between the administrative arrangements in the two provinces was that the Maharaja himself governed the Jammu province, while Kashmir was administered by a governor appointed by him. This may account for the feeling amongst the people of Kashmir province that the Maharaja did not regard them as "his own".[8] Moreover, Maharaja gave attention towards the modernisation of armed forces on the style of British army and stationed the troops all over the country. However, the army consisted almost entirely of Dogras, Dards and Punjabis and there were practically no Kashmiris, Balties and Ladakhis in the army. According to Kaul, "The Kashmiris were disqualified for military services".[9] The fact was that the Ranbir Singh like his father wanted to exclude every community (except his own) from his army and the high offices in the state. Thus, the Dogras have established a sort of Dogra imperialism in the state in which they enjoyed all the top positions and non-Dogra communities and classes were given place of subordination in the Dogra rule. No less devastative for the common Kashmiris was the exploitative taxation policy of the state which robbed the peasant of his produce leaving him to battle for survival.

Notwithstanding that the services offered by the Indian princes to the British Empire during the revolt of 1857 considerably shaped the colonial policy towards the princely states, abandoning the Dalhousie's policy of annexation.[10] However, the fact remains that with the passage of time a strong lobby emerged in British India which not only opposed the appeasing policy of the colonial state towards the princely states but even advocated the annexation of such states. The British policy towards Kashmir was no exception. However, the strategic importance of Kashmir in the geopolitics of the region made the British more attentive towards it who now eagerly wanted to control its internal affairs and therefore, devised ways of imposing the resident on the Dogra state, although there was no provision for resident in the treaty of Amritsar[11].

Not surprisingly therefore, when Ranbir Singh died on 14th September 1885 and Pratap Singh ascended the throne, 'Resident Political Officer' was appointed in the state.[12] It would not be out of place to mention that the British justified the imposition of the resident by highlighting the wretched condition of the Muslim masses in the state. With the appointment of the resident, the mixed court appointed by the British in 1872[13] was abolished and the Resident with his assistants were invested with powers to dispose of civil suits in which the parties were British Subjects or Indian Subjects of his Majesty.[14] The appointment of a resident in Kashmir was a necessary prelude to the implementation of wide-ranging reforms in the Dogra state. These included the introduction of a lighter assessment of revenue to be collected preferably in cash; the revision of existing taxes; the abolition of the system of revenue farming; the cessation of state monopolies; and dues (especially transit and customs dues and taxes on various trades and profession); the introduction of a modern and salaried bureaucracy manned by qualified individuals; a reorganisation of the Army which was also to be paid regular salaries; a system of proper financial control; improvements in the judicial administration of the state; the construction of proper roads; and the removal of all restrictions upon emigration.[15]

Giving the Maharaja face-saving device, the British Indian Government agreed to leave the initiation of such reforms to him and provided a liberal time-frame within which to do so.[16] Reforms were demanded by the colonial government in the name of impressing upon the Kashmiri government its obligation to its own subjects[17] and it was made clear that the Maharaja would not be permitted to shirk these. The Resident was to act as a watchdog on behalf of British government as well as of people in Kashmir, who were to see in his appointment an 'assurance of substantial reforms to come'.[18] As officially and publically justified, the installation of the Resident was in order to serve the interests of state subjects deeming to be suffering from a long and now intolerable history of misrule.[19] In this way the appointment and its rationale provided a heightened awareness among Kashmiri Muslims, a platform for the expression of their grievances. The number of petitions addressed to the Resident, rather than or in addition to the Kashmir government, proliferated dramatically from the end of the nineteenth century onwards.[20] Above all, measures were undertaken in the state under the British residency land settlement.

Although the powers of Pratap Singh were substantially curtailed by the British and the state was ruled over by the regency council set up under the patronage of the British resident. But Maharaja did not miss any opportunity to press upon the British for the restoration of his powers. However, after the restoration of his powers, the Maharaja was confronted with a new problem.Western educated men from the neighbouring Punjab and other places had been appointed in large numbers to the posts in administration. Kashmiris, who had hitherto been excluded from the affairs of the state, strongly resented this new encroachment from outside. Thus, Muslim subjects began to assume consciousness as they began to press for their rights.[21]

In 1921, Kashmiri Muslims strongly pleaded for appointments in government services and this was the beginning of political activity in Kashmir against the Dogra rule. However, Pratap Singh imposed ban on political activities and press in 1918 and no efforts were made to address the grievances of the common Kashmiris. The slogan 'state for the state's people' came to be heard everywhere but the Maharaja paid little heed to this growing movement. Neither the Maharaja nor his councilors then imagined that this demand of the people would one day lead to a strong agitation which would have to be faced by his successor and which would cost him his throne.[22]

The condition of Muslims in Kashmir, however, continued to be miserable and in 1924, they presented a memorandum to viceroy Lord Earl of Reading on his visit to Srinagar. This memorandum was regarding the land ownership rights, employment in state services, abolition of Begaar (Forced Labour) and handing over of mosques which were in the possession of Dogra Government.[23]

Shri Pratap Singh died in 1925 and was succeeded by his nephew Hari Singh, the only son of his brother Amar Singh. During the reign of Maharaja Hari Singh, the political consciousness had dawned on the entire length and breadth of the sub-continent. As a result, a continuous struggle for freedom and democratisation of the administration also started in the state. It had its origin in the widespread discontentment among the Muslim masses that constituted majority of the total population of the state. They had very inadequate representation in the state services as well as in the economic and industrial life of the state.[24] The bulk of the main population was tillers, labourers and artisan classes which were an excellent target of exploitation by the richer sections of the society.

The policy of provisional discrimination during Maharaja Hari Singh's time became very acute and during the time period of 1925 to 1931, the educated Kashmiris carried agitation for the freedom of press, right to form associations, establishment of representative legislature and proper representation of the people in the state administration. However, during the reign of Maharaja Pratap Singh, an agitation with the slogan 'state for state people' had started; this agitation grew stronger as the time went by. The outcome of this agitation was that on 31st January 1927,[25] "Heredity State Subject" was formed and passed into a law by Hari Singh which provided that 'Mulkis' (state subjects) would be preferred to outsiders in cases of employment in Government services. According to this subject, "All persons born as residing in state before the commencement of the reign of Maharaja Gulab Singh Bahadur and also persons who settled there in before the commencement of Samvat 1942 (1885 A.D.) and have since been permanently residing in Jammu and Kashmir are hereditary subjects of the state". In this order, Maharaja also put a ban on purchase of land by non-residents and also stopped the recruitment of Punjabis in the state services. But this order could not equally benefit all sections of people in the state because of Hari Singh's pro-Dogra policy. The people of Jammu, particularly Rajputs, got jobs while Pundits were appointed as clerks in offices vacated by the Punjabis. But needless to say that Muslims were still out of the picture.[26]

By 1930, the Kashmir had met with good number of educated young Muslims who had received higher education in different parts of India. During their educational life they were influenced by various movements which were launched by Indian leaders against the British government in Indian subcontinent. When they completed their education and returned back to home, they faced injustice, unemployment and felt frustrated. The young batch of educated Muslims started a Reading Room near Fatah Kadal in Srinagar. They used it to discuss their problems and they were convinced that the government was not willing to trust the Muslims by throwing open to them the doors of administration and removing various types of hurdles in their way. They were convinced that these rules and regulations were formed with the intention of keeping them away from administration.[27] On September 1930, Reading Room Party submitted a representation to the cabinet government and made the members familiar about the problem of unemployment faced by Muslims. On 6th October 1930, cabinet government invited a deputation of Reading Room Party to discuss the matter. Meanwhile, Sheikh Mohammad Abdullah and Abdul Aziz Fazali went to attend the meeting. After a long debate and discussion, Sheikh warned the cabinet government that they must face the consequences in case government showed any laziness in protecting the rights of Muslims of Kashmir.[28]

In the early 1931, a number of incidents took place in the states which were related with the Muslims that disturbed the religious sentiments of Muslim community within and outside the state. Historically and politically, 13th July 1931 is the most important day in the annals of the contemporary Kashmir. From this day, the struggle for independence and freedom in most modern sense started openly. Doubtless in 1931, the struggle was aggressively communal outward but those who had not kept their eyes shut could see that it was in essence. The struggle of victimized and enslaved prepare against the despotic rule. It was sooner or later bound to proceed on the right track.[29] Prem Nath Bazaz and a number of Kashmiri Pundits soon realised that the movement was spontaneous and expressed the inner urge of the downtrodden, tyrannised and suppressed millions under the autocratic alien Dogra rule. They therefore decided to attempt to drastically change the attitude of the Pundit community and meanwhile to become critical supporters of the freedom movement started by the masses.[30]

In September 1931, disturbances broke out in Kashmir province and resulted in the killings of some Kashmiri Muslims in Sopore, Baramulla, Shopian and Islambad townships. On 28th September 1931, a week after the Muslim agitation was restarted, the Government of India gave a warning to Maharaja Hari Singh asking him to take immediate steps to redress the grievances of the Muslims of the state and institute an enquiry commission headed by the British officer into the causes of the disturbance in the state. The Muslims of the Poonch and Mirpur rose in open conflict against the Dogras. Maharaja became helpless and accepted the orders of the Government of India and requested them for the military assistance in affected areas to restore law and order.[31]

The ruthlessness of the government did not deter the people of the state from continuing their struggle. However, when the Maharaja found that despite all his repressive machinery, the movement could not be crushed; he announced a general amnesty and proclaimed that if any section of his subjects desired to submit its reasonable demands, they would receive sympathetic consideration. Following this announcement, several memorials were submitted to the Maharaja by members of the different communities. Although different in many respects, the memorials had at least one common feature – the demand for the representative assembly and a system of government by an executive of ministers.[32] The Muslim memorial listed a number of grievances and demanded an increase in their representation in the public services in accordance with the percentage of the population. Added to this was the demand of perfect equality of rights and equality of treatment for all state subjects. The Maharaja considered these demands very carefully and sympathetically because of the fierce political unrest in the state.[33] Maharaja Hari Singh set up a committee to enquire into grievances and to make such recommendations as it deemed necessary. The Commission under the chairmanship of Mr. B. J. Glancy began its sittings in Srinagar. In the middle of January 1932, the Commission left Srinagar and moved down to Jammu. The Commission enquired into the complaints and grievances of the different communities and submitted its report to his Highness, Maharaja Bahadur on 22nd March, 1932. A series of reforms were made to the administrative structure and the system of education, land tenure and taxation in order to make life somewhat more bearable for the Muslim masses and provide opportunities to the small but increasingly vocal stratum of educated, angry young men that were advancing demands on their behalf. The Commission also urged that minimal freedoms of the press and public expressions should be tolerated. Some limited, halting action on the Glancy proposals was undertaken in the following years.[34]

Meanwhile, Jammu and Kashmir's first political party *'All Jammu and Kashmir Muslim Conference'* was founded in October 1932 to direct the emerging and growing movement for social and political change. Its principal leaders were Sheikh Abdullah from Kashmir and Chaudhary Gulam Abas from Jammu.[35] The people were now able to air their grievances from the platform of the Muslim Conference. The Conference protested against Maharaja for his failure to implement the recommendations of the Commission but no notice was taken of the complaint. In the same year, the Conference sent another commemorative to the Maharaja demanding 'responsible government' but as was expected, Maharaja refused to consider this request. Muslim Conference then called on the people to observe a 'responsible government day'. The day was observed but very few non-Muslims participated. Sheikh Abdullah therefore decided to seek non-Muslim support. He appealed to the non-Muslims to join hands with the Muslim Conference to fight against the autocracy of the Maharaja and remarked that the Muslim Conference was a party for every community.[36]

Secularisation of Kashmir Politics and Accession with India

On 28th June, 1938, a meeting of the working committee of the Muslim Conference was held in which Sheikh Abdullah moved a resolution suggesting to change the name of the Muslim Conference to National Conference and to amend the constitution so as to throw its doors open to non-Muslims. A special session of the All Jammu and Kashmir Muslim Conference was held at the Pather Masjid, Srinagar on 10th and 11th June 1938, which was attended by one hundred seventy eight delegates out of the two hundred that was the total strength of the general council.[37]

The special session was presided by Khawaja Gulam Mohammad Sadiq. In this special session, G. M. Sadiq declared that the party had always fought for Hindu Muslim unity, and assured that the session will be extending the jurisdiction of Muslim Conference to accommodate all the subjects of the state. Thus, a resolution was passed by the working committee of the Muslim Conference in its meeting held on June 1938, resolves that, in future the name of this conference will be the 'All Jammu and Kashmir National Conference'.[38] The resolution was passed by a majority of seventeen against three votes. This change in the nomenclature and the constitution of Muslim Conference enabled the Hindus and Sikhs to join the freedom struggle.This special session also resolved that every man and woman could become its member, irrespective of religion, caste, race and colour. This led to the secularisation of Kashmir politics.[39]

The National Conference decided to observe August 5, 1938, as the 'Responsible Government Day'. The day was observed all over the country and meetings were attended by a very large number of people of all communities. The meetings passed a resolution which reads, "This meeting of the people places on record its complete repudiation of the present system of irresponsible government and wishes to express its faith in the establishment of complete responsible government; which alone can cure the ills of the people".[40] These meetings alarmed the Maharaja. He realised that,"the people of his state were now united and that he could no longer suppress the rising public feeling". According to Prem Nath Bazaz, "some Muslim members expressed misgivings that a secular organisation would gravitate towards the Indian National Congress, the party leading India's independence movement and that the Hindu-Sikh elements in the party would undermine the freedom movement because of their vested interests in the Dogra rule. These fears, also voiced in 1939 by some of Abdullah's close colleagues, were allayed by an off-the-record understanding that the movement would steer of both the Congress and the All India Muslim League".[41]

In the beginning of 1940, All India Muslim League adopted the Pakistan Resolution headed by Ali Mohammad Jinnah and raised the slogan for creation of separate home land for Muslims in India. In its response, all the senior leaders of National Conference including Chowdary Abbas, Chowdary Ahmadulla and Allah Rakha Sagar supported the resolution and placed their support to the struggle for a separate home land for Indian Muslims.[42] In early 1941, Sardar Gawhar Rehman, a senior leader of Muslim Conference, travelled the state and worked for consolidation of the Muslim Conference and made an appeal to all Muslim organisations to help in the revival of the Muslim Conference in the state. A number of Muslim leaders went to Jammu to meet Chowdhary Abbas to revive the Muslim Conference in the state. Thus, it was in 1941 that the conservative Muslims in Kashmir, led by Chowdhary Abbas, revived the Muslim Conference in Kashmir. Both these political organisations, the Muslim Conference and the National Conference, intensified their campaigns.[43] The National Conference held its annual session on 29th and 30th September, 1944, at Sopore in Kashmir. The delegates to the session unanimously approved a manifesto namely the "New Kashmir Manifesto" which was divided into two parts: (1) The Constitution of the State and (2) The National Economic Plan.[44]

However, in 1946, National Conference launched the Quit Kashmir Movement to transfer power to the people. The state bureaucracy was bewildered at this new slogan and full of vengeance decided to crush the movement. Inspite of that, the movement was on the verge of success when the British rulers decided to divide Indian sub-continent into the new dominions of India and Pakistan in August 1947, and making all princely states independent and advising the Princes to accede to one or the other of the dominions, keeping in view the considerations of geographical contiguity.[45] The choice before Jammu and Kashmir State was a different one because partition of India makes Jammu and Kashmir state geographically bordering to both India and Pakistan besides Tibet, Sinkiang, USSR and Afghanistan. Moreover, the State of Jammu and Kashmir was a Muslim majority state with a Hindu ruler will get incline towards India. A majority of the inhabitants of the state were Muslim by religion. Thus, Pakistan thought that the state must accede to Pakistan.[46]

Maharaja Hari Singh found himself in a tight corner. Previously he had been averse to parting with an iota of power, but now he had seriously to consider the three alternatives: accession to India, accession to Pakistan and independence. He disliked the idea of becoming part of India which was being democratised, or of Pakistan which was a Muslim State. He thought independence and offered to sign a Standstill Agreement with both India and Pakistan aimed at continuing the existing relationship pending his final decision regarding the future of the state. But India did not accept the Standstill Agreement.[47]

A few weeks before the transfer of power in August 1947 a tribal invasion from Pakistan took place. These tribals have occupied some areas of Kashmir like Muzaffarabad, Bimbar, Kotll etc. It was felt that they would occupy the entire state and Maharaja Hari Singh also realised that he could no longer retain his hold over Kashmir; he fled from Kashmir to Jammu on 25th October 1947. He sought help from India Government and offered accession to it. Thus, State of Jammu and Kashmir acceded to India on 26th October, 1947, with only three subjects i.e., foreign affairs, communication and defence.[48]

After the accession, Maharaja Hari Singh was advised by the Government of India to constitute an Interim Government and invite the leaders of National Conference to join it. The decision to install Interim Government was put off for the time being. Pending the decision to appoint the Interim Government, Maharaja Hari Singh was persuaded to institute an emergency administration to deal with the instability caused by the tribal invasion. It was agreed upon that emergency administration would be headed by the President of the National Conference, Sheikh Mohammad Abdullah.[49] By a proclamation issued on March 5, 1948, Maharaja decided to replace the emergency administration by a popular Interim Government and provide for its powers, duties and functions, pending in the formation of a fully democratic constitution. Sheikh Abdullah was appointed as Prime Minister of the State of Jammu and Kashmir.[50] Negotiations on the provisions in the proposed Constitution of India that would embody the terms of the state's membership of the Union began when a conference of National Conference leader's and the Centre was held in Delhi on May 15 and 16, 1949. Pundit Nehru recorded the issues discussed in letter to Sheikh Sahib on 18th May. The state was having its own Constitution and "it will be for the Constituent Assembly of the state, when convened, to determine in respect of what other subjects the state may accede".[51]

The Constituent Assembly adopted the Constitution of India on November 26, 1949 (Constituent Assembly Document; Vol. 12, p. 995). It repealed the Government of India Act 1935. Article 394 provides that most of its provisions would come into force from January 26, 1950. On November 25, 1949, Maharaja of Jammu and Kashmir made a proclamation declaring that "the Constitution of India shortly to be adopted by the Constituent Assembly of India shall in so far as it is applicable to the State of Jammu and Kashmir, govern the constitutional relationship between this state and the contemplated Union of India.[52] On January 26, 1950 the President of India made the first constitution (Application to Jammu and Kashmir) order 1950 under Article 370 of the Constitution of India, which gives a special status to Jammu and Kashmir.[53] The new government led by National Conference introduced its radical agenda of land reforms and other structural changes in the economy as envisaged in its New Kashmir Manifesto in 1950. The specific about this reform was that unlike rest of India, the landlords were not paid compensation for the excess land recovered from them. Apart from the land reforms, many other policies were introduced which had the impact of upsetting the position of those in privilege. The extension of educational opportunities for larger number of people, for instance, was to open up state employment, so far monopolised by the elite, to the new sections of the society. The impact of these changes could be seen in the political responses of the entrenched classes of Jammu who sought to define the loss of their privileges in regional terms.[54] Regional process started right after the initiation of the land reforms when the erstwhile rich landed class that had to suffer the loss of land (without getting compensation) projected it as anti-Jammu policy. The exemption of orchards from the effect of land reforms legislations, for instance, was seen as a pro Kashmir policy since most of the orchards were located in Kashmir.[55] The politics of regional divide was further boosted with the enlargement of the middle classes both in Jammu as well as in Kashmir. There was this peculiar context of the state's economy which while being flushed with money was simultaneously defined by its perpetual status of dependency upon the centre with no source of employment other than government jobs. The artificially enlarged state sector, therefore, not only became the source of intense competition but also a terrain for regional contestation among the three regions of the state.[56]

Notes

1. Zutshi, U. K. *Emergence of political awakening in Kashmir*, Manhor Publications, New Delhi,1986, p. 19.
2. Kaur, Ravinderjit, *Political awakening in Kashmir*, Ashish Publications, New Delhi, 1996, p. 2.
3. *National Archives of India*, Foreign Department, Secret, 28th January, 1848, No. 35 and K.W.

4. Kaul, G. L., *Kashmir through Ages*, Chronicle Publishing House, Srinagar, 1967, p. 112.
5. Notes on Jammu and Kashmir, *National Archive*, Foreign Political, 8 July, 1863, pp. 73-75.
6. Zutshi, U. K. *Emergence of political awakening in Kashmir*, Manhor Publications, New Delhi,1986, p. 50.
7. Justice Anand, A. S. *The Constitution of J&K: Its Development and comment*, Delhi Universal Book Traders, edition 2004, p. 13.
8. *Ibid;* pp. 13-14.
9. Kaul, G. L. *Kashmir through Ages*, Chronicle Publishing House, Srinagar, 1967, pp. 112-113.
10. The Doctrine of Lapse was an annexation policy purportedly devised by Lord Dalhousie, who was the Governor General for the British in India between 1848 and 1856. According to the Doctrine, any princely state or territory under the direct influence (*Paramountcy*) of the British East India Company, as a vassal state under the British Subsidiary System, would automatically be annexed if the ruler was either manifestly incompetent or died without a direct heir.
11. Zutshi, U. K. *Emergence of political awakening in Kashmir*, Manhor Publications, New Delhi, 1986, pp. 47-48.
12. *National Archives of India,* Foreign Department, Political A, October 1872, 1848, Nos. 374-377.
13. A note on the relationship between the state of Jammu and Kashmir and the chiefships and territories comprised in the Gilgit Political Agency, *Jammu and Kashmir Archives,* File No. 10-C-1919.
14. Kaur, Ravinderjit, *Political awakening in Kashmir*, Ashish Publications, New Delhi, 1996, p. 10.
15. *Ibid;* p. 6.
16. Letter from Government of India to Lord Randolph Churchill, Secretary of State for India, dated 19 October 1885, reproduced in William Digby, p. 129.
17. Kaur Ravinderjit, *Political awakening in Kashmir*, Ashish Publications, New Delhi, 1996, p. 10.
18. Letter from Resident in Kashmir to the Secretary to the Government of India, Foreign Department dated 6 September 1885, reproduced to William Digby, p. 135.
19. Letter from the Government of India to Lord Randolph Churchill, Secretary of State for India, reproduced in William Digby, p. 129.
20. Rai, Mridu, *Hindu Rulers and Muslim Subjects*, Permanent Black Publisher Delhi, 2004, p. 275.
21. Kaur, Ravinderjit, *Political awakening in Kashmir*, Ashish Publications, New Delhi, 1996, p. 10.

22. Justice Anand, A. S. *The Constitution of J&K: Its Development and comment*, Delhi Universal Book Traders, edition 2004, p. 28.
23. Rai, Mridu, *Hindu Rulers and Muslim Subjects*, Permanent Black Publisher, Delhi, 2004, p. 275.
24. Kapoor, M. L. *History of Jammu and Kashmir, The Making of the State*, Gulshan Books Publications, Srinagar, 2005, pp. 25-26.
25. Maharaja Hari Singh constituted a committee to define the term state subject submitted its report, according to this definition.
26. Bazaz, P. N. *The History of Struggle for freedom,* Kashmir Publishing House, New Delhi, 1955, p.140.
27. Kaul, Santosh, *Freedom struggle in Jammu and Kashmir*, Anmol Publications, New Delhi, 1990, p.18.
28. Khan, G. H. *Freedom in Kashmir 1931-1940*, Light and Life Publications, New Delhi, 1980, pp.122-124.
29. Bazaz, P. N. *The History of Struggle for freedom* Kashmir Publishing House New Delhi, 1955, p.147.
30. *Ibid;* pp. 147-148.
31. Kaul, Santosh, *Freedom struggle in Jammu and Kashmir*, Anmol Publications, New Delhi,1990, pp. 20-21.
32. *All India State People's Conference*, Kashmir, p. 7.
33. Justice Anand, A. S. *The Constitution of J&K: Its Development and comment*, Delhi Universal Book Traders, edition 2004, p. 32.
34. Puri, Balraj, *Editorial in Kashmir Affairs*, Vol. 111, No. 10, Delhi, March/ April 1961.
35. Rai, Mridu, *Hindu Rulers and Muslim Subjects*, Permanent Black Publisher Delhi, 2004, p. 275.
36. Singh, Khushwant, *Sheikh Mohammad Abdullah Flames of Chinar: An Autobiography*, Penguin books, New Delhi, 1983, pp. 49-50.
37. Bamzai, P. N. K. *History of Kashmir*, A Metropolitan Book Co. Pvt. Ltd., New Delhi, 1962, p. 162.
38. Rai, Mridu, *Hindu Rulers and Muslim Subjects*, Permanent Black Publisher, Delhi, 2004, p. 275.
39. Khan, G. H. *Freedom in Kashmir 1931- 1940*, Light and Life Publications, New Delhi, 1980, pp.367-377.
40. Justice Anand, A. S. *The Constitution of J&K: Its Development and comment*, Delhi Universal Book Traders, edition 2004, p. 39.
41. Bazaz, P. N. *The History of Struggle for freedom*, Kashmir Publishing House New Delhi, 1955, p.190.
42. Kaul, Santosh. *Freedom struggle in Jammu and Kashmir*, Anmol Publications New Delhi, 1990, p. 69.

43. Justice Anand, A. S. *The Constitution of J&K: Its Development and comment*, Delhi Universal Book Traders, edition 2004, p. 58.
44. *Ibid;* pp. 58-59.
45. Bhushan, Vidhya, *Jammu and Kashmir Politics: its Critical Aspects*, Yak publishing channel, Jammu, 2008, p. 32.
46. *Ibid;* p. 33.
47. Teng, M. K. *State Govt. and Politics, Jammu and Kashmir*, Sterling Publisher, New Delhi, p. 2.
48. Justice Anand, A. S. *The Constitution of J&K: Its Development and comment*, Delhi Universal Book Traders, edition 2004, p. 74.
49. *Ibid;* p. 75.
50. Teng, M. K. *State Govt. and Politics, Jammu and Kashmir*, Sterling Publisher, New Delhi, p. 10.
51. *State Autonomy Committee Report Government of Jammu and Kashmir*, April 1999, p. 18.
52. *Ibid;* pp. 18-19.
53. *White Paper on Indian States; Government of India, Ministry of States*, New Delhi, 1950, p. 371.
54. Behera, Navnita C. *Demystifying Kashmir,* Dorling Kindersley publisher, (India) Delhi, 2007, p.109.
55. *Ibid;* p. 111.
56. Om Hari and Rekha Chowdhary, (eds.) *Politics of Autonomy*, Vinod Publishers, Jammu, 1999, p.172.

Chapter - 2

Identity and Regional Aspirations in Jammu and Kashmir

Regionalism is a complex concept which has been defined in various ways by several social scientists. Some analysts define regionalism as a manifestation of 'World Federalism' and an intermediate state between administrative decentralisation and federalism. They advocate that politics of regionalism involves such diverse problems of modern political and cultural life as those of minorities, administrative decentralisation, local self-government, autonomy, the cult of homeland and slogans such as "sons of the soil" expressing local patriotism.[1]

Regionalism is the manifestation of particularising of various socio-cultural groups which is generated from a variety of factors such as geographical isolation, independent historical heritage, and racial, ethnic or religious loyalties.[2] Regionalism is indeed a dynamic and multi-dimensional concept. It encompasses geo-physical, psychological, socio-cultural and politico-economic variable. All these components cumulatively influence the growth of regionalism. However, regionalism is not always a negative phenomenon. From a positive angle, regionalism connotes a quest for self-identity and self-fulfillment on the part of a particular region vis-à-vis overall national development. Hence, the quest for regional identity is not always antithetical to the process of nation building.[3] Negatively, regionalism reflects a psyche of alienation from the national mainstream. This originates due to excessive centralisation and discriminative attitude of the ruling elite. In case the leaders and politicians in a given political system fail to accommodate various regional aspirations of various regions and sub-cultural groups, regionalism can certainly contribute to the overall national development and national integration. Thus, in order to provide a positive shape to regionalism much depends upon the policy-makers and the ruling elite who can hopefully maintain a balance between centrifugal and centripetal forces in a given system.[4]

However, regionalism grows when the people inhabiting a particular place inside a nation state feel that they are bound together by ties which are distinct from and stronger than the bonds which link them to other sections of the people living outside the region. Regionalism thus fosters among the people a sense of being a distinct territorial community with its own life and interests and inculcates in them a desire to organise themselves into a distinct political unit for the protection and promotion of their interests.[5] In fact, there are two types of determinants of regionalism, subjective and objective. The subjective components of regionalism are the way of life, customs and traditions, forms of art, language and literature, social heritage, beliefs, attitudes and values related to the group. The objective components of regionalism are territorial, regional and the environment complex within which the regional group lives. Taken together these subjective and objective components constitute the determinants of regionalism.[6]

The postmodern thought recognises two basic human urges: urge for identity and urge for unity. Both would be crushed in a forcible uniformed community. The process of modernisation, democratisations, information explosion and technological revolution, as universally acknowledged, sharpens urge for identity. Unity and identity are quite different things. Unity is international in references, international perspective and rooted in political feeling while as identity is local and regional, rooted in imagination and work of culture. National unity is a statement about politics; it is affirmed or challenged by political activities and the measure of its achievements ranges from political stability or instability, the absence or presence of commitment to the survival of the national political experiment.[7]

According to Balraj Puri, "regional and sub-regional consciousness is likely to grow with the process of modernisation and democracy". He thinks that, "technological revolution, instead of wiping out smaller identities, has led to restlessness, alienation and atomisation of the individuals. This vacuum is filled by his urge for identity which he seeks in smaller culture, language, group, history and region with which he identifies himself".[8]

Paul Wallace argued that historical and cultural environment of a region shapes the distinctive relationship between region and nation in India. He concludes that Indian civilisation and regional culture are the two realities of Indian federalism. This observation echoes the thoughts of many others.[9] Navnita Chadha Behera says that root cause of the regional alienation and suffering among different regions lie in the organisation of the nation- state. She argued that nation state itself is facing pressure from the regional and sub-regional levels and regional identity and regionalism involve many kinds of problems – social, cultural, political and historical. These aspects manifested in the demand for secession, demand for separate state, demand for regional autonomy, demand for state autonomy and Centre - state dispute.[10] The regionally based ethnic, tribal, cultural or religious subgroups have begun to make demands which at time border on separation. For instance, the United States of America because of the vastness of its size and multiplicity of cultural groups have engendered regional cleavages on many occasions. The civil war between the northern and southern states, fought for a long period of time, was one of the most remarkable inter-regional cleavages in the history of United States of America.[11]

In France, in spite of the polarisation of politics between left and right which has helped to moderate the process of the emergence of regional consciousness in many less developed regions like Lorraine, Occitania, Corsica and catholic regions like Brittany, regionalism is re-emerging and getting footholds.[12] In Italy, also the conflict between northern regions like Lombardy and Piedment which took the lead in industrialisation and the relatively less developed southern areas, especially Frulia, though not so strong yet, had definitely some impact on the Italian politics.[13] In West Germany, though politics is dominated by issues that cut across all regions, Bavaria still retains the strong regional identity and is conscious of economic and political dominance by the Rhine- Westphalia region. The union of the two Germanys after forty five years of separate and mutually hostile existence is likely to add another dimension to regionalism in united Germany.[14]

In Canada, the problem of regionalism is very serious in Quebec where economy is controlled by the Anglophones but numerically the region is dominated by Francophones. The Quebecois for the bias in the industrial development and consider the cause of their economic problems as a consequence of cultural division of the country and Anglophone dominance.[15] The question of regional identity in the Soviet Union involves non-Russian groups which constitute more than half of the Soviet population residing in different geographical regions. These include small tribal groups in remote areas, non-western people with ancient literary and artistic traditions such as the Uzbeks, large Slavic groups such as the Ukrainians, small but highly educated and advanced populations- as in the Baltic States which are closer to Central Europe on Scandinavia than to Moscow. The Soviet Union claimed to have resolved the vexed problem by granting cultural autonomy to these regions but the unilateral declaration of independence by Armania and Ukraine threaten the unity of the Soviet states.[16]

Regionalism is also one of the most common features of the politics of most of the Asian, African and Latin American countries, where lack of integration is evident among the several religious, cultural, ethnic or tribal groups which are generally regional based and are relatively autonomous, self-contained and traditionally hostile towards one another. Frequently, these groups are stratified within the state along social, economic and political lines, further complicating the problem of nation building because the different identities both cross cut and converge.[17] Above all, the problem of regionalism also assumes special importance in the context of third world countries because of the low level of socio-economic development, incompleteness of the process of class formation, the mixed character of the economy, characteristic of most of developing countries, the continuing dominance of foreign monopolies and the retention of many of the archaic forms and traditional institutions of pre-capitalist society.[18]

Regionalism is not a new phenomenon in the Indian political system. In the pre-independence days it was promoted by the British imperialists and they deliberately encouraged the people of various regions to think in terms of their region rather than the nation as a whole, with a view to maintain their hold over India. After independence, the leaders tried to foster a feeling among the people that they belonged to one nation. The framers of the Indian Constitution sought to achieve this by introducing single citizenship for all. With the same objective, a unified judiciary, all India services and a strong central government was provided.[19] However, in view of the vastness of the country and different cultures, regionalism soon made its appearance in India. The first vague manifestation of regionalism was the demand for reorganisation of states on linguistic basis. However, the most effective play of regionalism in India was the victory of the Drawida Munitra Kamaga (DMK) against Congress giants in Tamil Nadu in 1960's. Initially, the central leadership felt that regionalism was a peripheral political factor confined to Tamil Nadu and hence did not pose any threat to national unity.[20] However, these hopes were ill founded soon in Punjab, the Akali Movement gained momentum while in Jammu and Kashmir Sheikh Abdullah revived the National Conference. During these initial years, the all India political parties continued to adjust with these regional forces on the plea that they would ultimately succeed in making inroads into the bases of the regional parties and absorb in their organisations.[21]

The Indian National Congress which enjoyed monopoly of power (between 1947-1967) and followed a policy of blowing hot and cold towards the regional forces also contributed to the growth of regionalism in India. It accommodated the regional forces when convenient and raised a clamour against them when it was pitted against them. In fact, a close link developed between central and regional leadership which greatly encouraged the growth of regionalism.[22]

The concept of regionalism in Indian politics is generally regarded as something that is anti-system, anti-federal and against the basic interests of the well-integrated and well-developed polity. In Indian federation, the fight is actually between regional identities and national integrity and the point is how to have both. Regional identities are a reality of Indian federal polity and at the same time it would be unrealistic to expect total integration in a country where lies the diversity as India has. On political level, the rise of regionalism as a force cannot be ignored.[23] The wide variety of cultures and languages has given rise not only to different identities but also to a multiplicity of identities that an Indian generally possesses. What gives a particular significance to these identities is the fact that most of them are sociocultural meanings; thereby most of cultural identities are associated with the specific regions. The socio-cultural identities became a vehicle for political phenomenon called regionalism and sub-regionalism both of which are sub-group phenomenon, the main difference being of the level at which they manifest.[24]

In the Indian context and following Iqbal Narrain's typology, regionalism could be classified into three types. First is the supra state regionalism that refers to that manifestation of regionalism which cuts across state boundaries or in which states or parts are grouped together in terms of regional identity. The conflict between north and south India on the language issue and Jharkhand movement can be cited as examples of supra state regionalism. Second type of regionalism is called inter-state regionalism in which "the regional identity of one state is in competition with the regional identity of the other state mostly for economic development, sharing of benefits and allied purposes". The various movements and agitations involving the issues such as Maharashtra–Karnataka Border Dispute, river water dispute etc. are some of the examples. The third and final type of regionalism is characterised as intrastate regionalism that refers to a situation where a part of state develops the quest for self-identity and self-development, positively or negatively. It expresses a psyche of deprivation or exploitation in relation to other parts of the same state. This phenomenon is also called as sub-regionalism. Movements, however, for economic development and an anxiety for a proper share in political power, the Jammu and Kashmir fits this example.[25]

Regional Identities and Regional Consciousness in J&K

The concept of identity has captured the stage of social science. The identity aspirations and sense of identity have offered a new dimension to the assertiveness of ethnic groups. A sense of identity means a sense of being at one with oneself. It means, at the same time, a sense of affinity with a community's sense of being at one with its future as well as history or mythology.[26]

Identity formation in South and South-East Asian societies has followed a uniform pattern. These identities which evolved over a large span of time may be located in specific geographical and environmental spaces. They have the characteristics of a common language spoken by groups of people with a history of observing common traditions, rites and rituals. All these components have endowed these identities with an aura of primordiality. The prominent aspect of these identities has been their inclusiveness in absorbing new and sometimes even foreign influences of religions and cultures resulting in adding layer in the formation of their distinct personalities. The incorporation of shared historical and cultural values shaped these identities in a mold in which the religious edges of the identity remained subdued or even dormant. It is interesting to note that the capacity of absorption and accommodation of these identities resulted in two diametrically opposite consequences. At one level, these identities remained humane and inclusive, incorporating and reflecting broader human and universal values. Here at the other level, they acquired the traits of particularism which in the later stages of building multi-cultural and multi-ethnic nation states posed many problems.[27]

The state of Jammu and Kashmir is composed of three main regions- Jammu, Kashmir and Ladakh. The internal politics of the state marked by inter-regional tensions that have influenced the attitude of the people on the question of their external affiliations. On the other hand, the geo-political profile of the state clearly depicts its heterogeneity. The multiplicity of its ethnic, religion, linguistic–regional – cultural character as well as the growing identities and regional consciousness in the three regions - Jammu, Kashmir and Ladakh has also left a deep impact on the overall politics of the state. In each of the three regions of the state a different attitude on the issue of accession can be clearly noticed from the very day of state's accession to India.[28] As Hari Om says, "A sort of local nationalism had developed in all the three regions of the state".[29]

In Kashmir, People's alienation from the national identity has been a constant problem since long. They tend to give more importance to ethno religious and regional identities than to considerations of unified state and the nation.

Kashmiri Identity and Regional Consciousness

Kashmiri identity and its relationship with other identities- national, regional and sub-regional could be related to the foregoing formulations. Kashmir has the distinction of a recorded history of 5,000 years. Its identity, that has been described by scholars as '*Kashmiriyat*', evolved through the process of acculturation absorbing diverse cultural elements and accommodating different religious practices ranging from Buddhism, Shaivism, Jainism and Islam. These faiths, during varied periods of time, incorporated local customs and traditions within their respective folds, providing *Kashmiriyat* with distinct, inclusive and plural characteristics.[30] Kashmir has its own distinct variety of

Rishi order which is similar to the universal Sufi order of Islam, but has its roots within Kashmir. The special geographic location of Kashmir and a common language-*Kashmiri* as their mother tongue which bound the people of diverse faiths together and the social structure provided the *Kashmiriyat* with a distinct form, content and personality. The accommodation and tolerance remained the hallmarks of Kashmir identity.[31]

Moreover, Kashmir valley for a variety of reasons holds a pivotal position in the politics of the state. This is not solely because the rest of the world knows the state by this name and it has been presented nationally and internationally by Kashmiri speaking representatives, but also because Kashmiris have led all the government in the state since independence. Some of the unique features of Kashmir which make Kashmiris conscious of their unique identity include its geography, history, language, culture and civilisational heritage. Geographically, it has existed in splendid isolation, though internally well connected. Kashmir is the largest valley in the lap of the largest mountains in the world, ranging from 10,000 to 18,000 feet in height and they enclose a plain of around 1900 sq. miles. Kashmir also has an over six hundred years old recorded literary heritage.[32]

Moreover, several factors have contributed to a strong feeling of regional identity among the people of Kashmir valley. These factors - geographical, historical and political, served to unite Kashmiris as a political force under the leadership of Sheikh Mohammad Abdullah. The physical isolation of the Kashmir valley had also played an important role in the development of Kashmiri regionalism.[33] The remoteness of the Kashmir valley has further promoted a feeling of separation not only because it has discouraged the mass influx of new settlers but also because it has restricted Kashmiris contact with the outside world. Confinement to a relatively small area for generations has produced usual degree of cultural and racial homogeneity. The Kashmiris have developed a sense of community encompassing the majority Muslim population. Although remote and isolated, the Kashmir valley became a prised object of conquest for ambitious rulers of neighbouring kingdoms.[34]

Historically, the roots of present day Kashmiri identity and regional consciousness anxiety preservation date back to 1586 and 1846. Mughal Emperor Akbar eliminated the semi-independent Kashmiri principality as part of imposing direct Mughal rule throughout the state empire and the later when Kashmir was sold to Dogra Maharaja Gulab Singh in the Treaty of Amritsar. The Mughals, as a colonial power, tried to psychologically ostracize Kashmiris during their rule.[35] The founding of Dogra rule in the aftermath of 1846 brought about the creation of a new system of agrarian exploitation, a parasitic urban growth based upon it. The land grants-jagirs and Chaks–assumed institutionalised form. The new polity combined political authority and economic power. However, the clash between Kashmiri identity and Dogra usurpation was noticeable when the treaty met with an uprising. At the time when political consciousness started taking shape in Kashmir, the condition of both the peasantry as well as the class of artisans was pathetic. Walter Lawrence, the settlement officer of the time recorded that when he started settlement of land, everything, say air and water was under taxation. The most oppressive was the system of Begar (forced labour).[36] Kashmir witnessed a number of movements throughout the twentieth century–in the 1910s, 1920s and 1930s. Representing the interests of the lower classes, these movements intensified Kashmiri yearning for fulfilling their emerging sense of national feeling and 1931 was the culminating point in that.[37]

The Kashmiri identity, however, was marked by the political movement which started in July 1931 against the Dogra monarchy. The entire cause of this movement and its vicissitudes can broadly be interpreted in terms of the urge of the Kashmiri nationalists to seek avenues of self-awareness, self-expression, self-assertion and self-determination.[38] As a result of this, political awakening in Kashmir expressed itself in the form of Muslim consciousness through an informal political form as the Muslim Conference in 1932 under the leadership of Sheikh Mohammad Abdullah. Such Muslim consciousness demanded more government jobs for Muslims, democratic rights, freedom of expression and association and political power through responsible government. As the ruler was a Dogra Hindu, non-Kashmiri and non-Muslim, the demand of democracy satisfied regional and religious urges of the Kashmiri masses. The change of the Muslim Conference into All Jammu and Kashmir National Conference in 1939 not only secularised the Kashmir politics but also invited non-Muslims valuable support to the democratic government in the state under the charismatic leadership of Sheikh Muhammad Abdullah.[39]

However, regional consciousness in Kashmir took a new turn after the accession of the state to the Indian union in 1948-49. Moreover, Sheikh Abdullah abolished monarchy and landlordism. As a result of this, most of the people of Jammu looked upon the party as a manifestation of militant Kashmiri nationalism. Also, the Kashmir leaders have attached more importance to maximum autonomy for Kashmir. Sheikh Abdullah stated that many Kashmiris were apprehensive that if special status for Kashmir was not granted in the Indian Constitution how he could convince the Kashmiris that India does not interfere in the internal affairs of Kashmir. He said, "If our right to shape our destiny is challenged and if there is resurgence of communalism in India, how are we to convince the Kashmiris that such development might lead to merger of their distinct identity".[40] Sheikh Abdullah's stress on distinct identity of Kashmir ultimately resulted in his arrest and dismissal on August 9, 1953. After Sheikh Abdullah's arrest, Mirza Afzal Beg through Plebiscite Front urged upon the powers at the helm of affairs to keep the Kashmiri identity intact. It espoused the cause of self-determination of the Kashmiris through a plebiscite under the United Nations auspices and withdrawal of forces of India and Pakistan from Kashmir. On April 13, 1958, Sheikh Abdullah sent a letter to the Prime Minister of India Jawaharlal Nehru, asking him to grant the people of Kashmir their right to self-determination; otherwise he was sure that the conscience of the world would force India to yield to their demand. Similarly in 1960, Sheikh Abdullah wrote to a sympathizer in London, "ever since 1931, when the national movement was launched, our idea had been a right of self-determination for the people of Kashmir, and to that end I am contributing my humble bit.[41] This right of self-determination is a universally recognised right, and is the sheet anchor of the United Nations Charter. Yet, Kashmiri people are today suffering incalculable hardships for the achievement of this right, otherwise conceded to every nation".[42]

Similarly at the annual session of the Plebiscite Front at Sopore in November 1964, Sheikh Abdullah said, "it was meaningless to argue in a negative way that a Kashmir solution was possible only when India and Pakistan agreed to it. The right to decide their destiny belongs to Kashmiri people and no power, however mighty, could deny it to them. It was because of the fact that the people of Kashmir had not exercised their right that there had been no settlement".[43] In December 1964, Sheikh Abdullah also sent a memorandum to the Prime Minister of India demanding self-determination for the people of Kashmir. Sheikh Abdullah, however, reacted unfavourably to the extension of Articles 356[44], 357[45] of Indian constitution and the merger of the National Conference into Indian National Congress. In a speech delivered on January 15, 1965, at Hazratbal Srinagar, he appealed directly to Kashmiris to oppose the applications of Articles 356, 357 and to resist the impositions of the Congress Party on Kashmir.[46] Those who were working for the merger of the National Conference with the Indian National Congress were dubbed enemies of Kashmir and Sheikh Abdullah asked his audience to boycott them completely. The formation of the Congress Party in the state was not to bring freedom to Kashmiris in the state but to tighten the chains of slavery on them. The simmering revolt continued to agitate the Kashmiris and by March 7, 1965 the situation became explosive enough to warrant a large scale arrest of the leaders of the Plebiscite Front.[47] Sheikh Abdullah convened J&K People's Convention which was held at Mujahid Manzil in Srinagar from October 12, 1968 on-words. The proposals and discussions in the State People's Convention reveal that it was about to seek Kashmiri identity separate from India and Pakistan. Almost similar views were expressed in the second convention which was held on June 8, 1970, in Srinagar. The feeling of preserving Kashmiri identity was also echoed in the Kashmir Accord, wherein it was agreed that any law extending the powers of Union Parliament over the state after 1953 on any matter could be alterable in the concurrent list, encroaching Kashmiri identity.[48]

During 1977 State Assembly elections, the National Conference was challenged by the Janta Party which had become a common front of all anti-National Conference elements in the state. Sheikh Abdullah condemned the Janta party as an outside party led by an outside leadership which would threaten the distinct identity of the Kashmir. The main Plank of Sheikh Abdullah's election campaign was the preservation of Kashmiri identity, an objective he had failed to secure in the Kashmir Accord. Unable to campaign due to illness, he recorded a cassette with the message that the election was a referendum on Kashmir's self-respect that they could now show the world they are master of their destiny and the central government could not dictate their future.[49] The wave of Kashmiri regionalism put aside all other issues and swept National Conference to power with 39 out of 42 seats in the Kashmir valley and Sheikh Abdullah again took the charge of the state government on July 9, 1977.[50]

After the demise of Sheikh Abdullah on 1982, his son Farooq Abdullah was appointed Chief Minister of Jammu and Kashmir State. In his first address to the National Conference legislative party, Farooq Abdullah declared that he was a Kashmiri, would remain a Kashmiri and would die a Kashmir.[51] In the 1983 State Assembly election, the National Conference projected itself as spokesman of Kashmiri regionalism. Its manifesto portrayed late Sheikh Abdullah as a symbol of the hopes and aspirations of Kashmiri people. In its outcome, the National Conference came to be identified with the Kashmir valley when it won 38 out of 42 seats. Subsequently, the dismissal of Farooq Abdullah's government on July 2, 1984, hurt the regional aspirations of the Kashmiri people. It had caused strong resentment among the Kashmiri people against the Centre, Congress (I) party and those who defeated and formed a minority government in the state. The Kashmir valley remained tense and reeled under violence for certain months.[52]

Later on, people of Kashmir also opposed the Rajiv-Farooq Accord of 1986. They felt that Rajiv-Farooq Accord would bring nothing but dishonour to the Kashmiris. In 1987 Assembly Election, Kashmiriyat was mobilised by a coalition of Islamic groups known as Muslim United Front (MUF). The Muslim United Front's focus of campaign was again on Kashmiri identity.[53] Periodic demands for state autonomy and revision of the 1953 status were emanation from Farooq Abdullah and his political party National Conference for participating in elections. Keeping this in view, the Prime Minister of India P.V. Narashima Rao announced in 1995 that sky is the limit in conceding autonomy to Jammu and Kashmir state. But Farooq Abdullah placed stringent conditions for participating in elections.[54] The National Conference demanded a return of the same degree of autonomy as it existed before 1953 and a substantial economic package for the State of Jammu and Kashmir. When this did not happen, National Conference boycotted the Parliamentary poll in May 1996. Roots of separatist crisis in the state could be safely traced back to Farooq's dismissal in July 1984. This exposed the myth of National Conference's capacity (within the given constitutional framework) to secure what it had been promising to the people of the state i.e. to regain the position that it had lost since

1953.[55] It was during the Governor's rule (1986 to 1987) that the extremist trends in Kashmir politics started emerging and gaining strength. The parties which proved secular or nationalist credentials like the National Conference started losing ground and new forces with more non-secular shade started gaining popular support in the valley. These forces grouped together under the banner of the Muslim United Front (MUF).[56] Making Dr. Farooq Abdullah to submit to the central government through an alliance between him and the party in power in Delhi totally undermined him and his capacity of representing the distinctive Kashmiri sentiments and the identity urges of the people there. In other words, it blocked the normal and moderate channels of expression of Kashmiri sentiments, thereby having the way for new forces to replace them as vanguards of the people and their interests in the state. This situation helped in strengthening the Muslim United Front to make it a major force in Kashmir politics. So much so, National Conference-Congress Alliance had to resort to large scale rigging in order to secure clear majority in the State Assembly and prevent Muslim United Front (MUF) from winning a respectable number of seats in the State Assembly.[57] By doing so, a golden opportunity of exercising an influence of moderation on the MUF was missed by denying it an opportunity of participation in the democratic process and thereby co-opting it into the system. Instead, this exposed the National Conference-Congress alliance further and people got completely alienated from Indian national mainstream.[58] This particularly cost the National Conference very heavily, as it proved undoing of its all past glory and undermined its future chances. Most important of all, the people in general and the youth in particular in Kashmir lost faith even in democracy. The younger generation felt that in order to get justice the only alternative open to them was to resort to armed violence. More significantly the issue went beyond autonomy and it has marked the resurgence of the separatist movement in the valley.[59]

After the eruption of militancy in 1990, the Indian Government promised autonomy once again. The objective behind this was to check the secessionist trend in Kashmir and create a favourable situation in 1996 for the pro-accession parties and hold the elections. Though the situation was not favourable, yet the dates for the parliamentary elections were fixed. The major regional and pro-accession party of the state, the Jammu and Kashmir National Conference threatened to boycott these elections as its President Farooq Abdullah insisted that the quantum of Autonomy should be decided before the polls. However, the Central Government remained adamant that the question of autonomy would be decided with the elected representatives of the state.[60] Farooq Abdullah, after winning the assembly elections in 1996, concentrated on his party's priority of defining, deciding and negotiating a package of Autonomy for the state and, within this package of Autonomy, the quantum of Regional Autonomy for the three regions of the state. It was with this intention that the Government of Jammu and Kashmir passed the Autonomy resolution in 2001. But this resolution was turned down by the Bhartiya Janta Party led National Democratic Alliance (NDA) Government at the Centre. This negative attitude of the central government towards the restoration of the autonomy of the state strengthened the belief of Kashmiris that any sort of political solution is a distant dream. It also made the National Conference which had been an ally in the NDA Government at the Centre, to pay a high price in 2002 Assembly elections. In these elections the National Conference was voted out of power and a Congress–Jammu and Kashmir Peoples Democratic Party (PDP) coalition government was formed in the state.[61]

Jammu Identity and Regional Consciousness

The identities in Jammu region share common ethno-cultural and even to some extent linguistic traditions. Moreover, they share the regional contiguity. The Jammu identity suffered a severe jolt when parts of the territory which shared the ethno-cultural-linguistic traditions with this region, particularly Muzaffarabad and Poonch, were occupied by Pakistan and are now known as Pak Occupied Kashmir. Jammu is, in many respects, a contrast with Kashmir. It is not geographically closed and compact.[62] Far from being a melting pot of faiths and races as Kashmir is, it is a mosaic. It did receive new faiths and ethnic communities but far from merging them into single entity as Kashmir did, it accommodated them as distinct separate identities.

Its plural society, almost entirely of Aryan stock, included 66 per cent Hindu, 30 per cent Muslims and 6 per cent Sikhs. Three out of ten districts (census 2001) adjoining Kashmir region namely, Rajouri, Poonch and Doda have Muslim majority. Though languages of the region belong to a single family of languages Dogri, Gojri, Pahari and Punjabi are the principal languages of the region besides a number of other dialectics.[63] It comprises the districts of Kathua and Jammu and Hindu majority tehsils in Udhampur and Doda districts, geographically contiguous with Kathua and Jammu districts. The Jammu plains are situated at an altitude of 300 to 600 meters above sea level and the Shivalik hills lying towards the north of these plains have an altitude of 600 to 1800 meters. The dress pattern, food pattern, architecture, customs, traditions and the belief system of the majority community, i.e., the Hindus of this region resemble the north Indian states. However, the identity movement from Jammu can be traced from 1820 to 1947 when the Jammu region was homeland of the ruling dynasty, as the autocratic rulers of the state belonged to the Dogra community.[64] In 1857 as well as the Second World War, the Dogra rulers supported the British to crush the revolt against imperialism in India and abroad. The last autocratic Dogra ruler of the state, Maharaja Hari Singh was throughout averse to the plans of the Indian National Congress and Jammu and Kashmir National Conference to forge constitutional ties of Jammu and Kashmir with the Indian union to safeguard the sovereignty of the state as well as his dynastic rule over Jammu and Kashmir.[65]

During the freedom struggle in Kashmir, the Dogras of Jammu identified themselves with loyalty towards Dogra ruler Maharaja Hari Singh. They considered that their rights and interests would be more protected at the hands of Hindu ruler against the chauvinistic politics of the majority community. But in post-independence period, when monarchy was abolished, the Dogras of Jammu looked towards India for the protection of their interests and social security against the domination of Kashmiri chauvinism. The political identity movement in the Jammu region was founded by Mahatma Budh Singh who resigned from what was then a very prestigious post of Deputy Commissioner to form Kisan Mazdoor Sabha in 1925, fourteen years before the National Conference was formed in Kashmir. Dogra Sabha was the first non-official organisation formed in 1905 by Lala Hans Raj.[66] In 1931, when Budh Singh became its President, it acquired a political character. However, when the National Conference of Kashmir was recognised by the Congress as its counterpart in the state, the secular progressive movement in Jammu was split. Though Budh Singh continued to be in the National Conference, many Hindu and Muslim leaders of Jammu found it difficult to sell the battle cry of Kashmir National Conference viz. Dogra Raj Murdabad to Dogra dominated Jammu region. The Hindu Maha Sabha and Muslim Conference were quick to own them respectively. In 1947, both of them supported the urge for independence of the state being nourished by Maharaja with whom they shared a common regional and ethnic identity.[67]

A faster and more pronounced form of regional consciousness in Jammu took after 1947. Partly it was due to a reaction against the dominating position of Kashmiri leadership in the post-independence power structure of the state and for more homogenous and distinctive nature of Kashmir personality with 94 per cent Muslims and nearly 90 per cent Kashmiri speaking population - which automatically carved out regional identities on it's either side; further separating it from Jammu by the geographical barrier of the Pirpanchal range and from Ladakh by the Zojila.[68] The process of modernisation, politicisation and democratisation was also responsible for enhancing a sense of regional self-awareness. The clash between the Jammu and Kashmir has apparently been communal and ideological for they are different not only in language and culture but also in their predominate religion. In Jammu region there is a political discourse that revolves around the issues related to regional deprivation and neglect. Kashmir in this discourse forms the centre of power within the state and is perceived to be dominating not only the power structure of the state but also controlling the economic and material resources. It is on this basis that the popular perceptions have been articulated around the concept of regional imbalances and a number of agitations have been organised in Jammu. The National Conference essentially represented the regional patriotism of Kashmir valley.[69] It had confined its activities to the Kashmir region mainly because it was inhibited by its basic philosophy i.e. regional patriotism of Kashmir. Moreover, Kashmiri leadership did not have much contact with and trust in Jammu workers of their party which functioned in an ad hoc manner with repeated changes in the composition of its committees at various levels in the region. The important group of Chaudhari Ghulam Abbas was the first to leave the National Conference, not long after it was formed. As a unified and composite leadership of the whole state could not grow, the dominant urges of its two principal regions started diverging.[70] The growth of regional consciousness in Jammu after independence was sharp and fast. The political and administrative setup in the state after the linkup between the state and the Indian union brought about in 1947, proved conducive to regional tensions. A glaring feature of the situation was that ever since the advent to power of National Conference in 1948, political power in the state had been vested almost exclusively in Kashmir politicians and Jammu was relegated virtually to a subsidiary position.[71]

The people of Jammu also alleged that leaders of National Conference, who wielded at that time maximum political power without any external control, never thought it prudent to share this power with the Jammu region. They looked towards Delhi for more and more power; being quite aware of the fact that valley is nucleus of India's secularist conception of the state. One solid and sound reason to safely deprive Jammu from sharing any political power, at that time was the National Conference's Programme of distributing thousands of acres of land, seized from the Dogra Hindu absentee-landlords which was to be given free of cost to the landless tenants. No compensation was paid to those whose land was confiscated. This annoyed the affected landowners of Jammu province and resulted in their antagonistic political behaviour. Thus, the causes of Jammu being alienated from the politics of the Kashmir valley are deep rooted, with the result that both the regions adopted a definite political line of action divergent to each other against the oneness of state.[72] Therefore, in November, 1948, Dogras of Jammu found the Praja Parishad Party to advocate the lost cause of Hindu supremacy in state politics and administration which held sway before. The formation of the Praja Parishad was welcomed by the masses of Jammu because at that time there was a feeling of deprivation among the people of Jammu and it began to spread very fast. It was destined to come with conflict with the state government seeking social justice. The main object of the Praja Parishad was to achieve full integration of the state with the rest of the India like other princely states and safeguard the legitimate rights of the people of Jammu from the government of Sheikh Abdullah.[73]

Constituent Assembly dominated by the National Conference had created unitary state with a clear concentration of powers in the valley through disproportionate representation in both the Constituent Assembly and the State Assembly.[74] With 45 per cent of the state's total population and a land area of 26,293 sq. km, Jammu was substantially larger than the valley that covers 15,853sq. km. Yet Jammu had only thirty two members in the state Legislative Assembly compared with forty four of the valley. Also, the Kashmir Valley returned one member for 73,000 inhabitants whereas Jammu returned one for 90,000 inhabitants. In parliamentary elections, Jammu returned one member for 1.4 million people compared with one member for one million people in the valley. Ladakh's 95,876 sq. km constituted sixty percent of the state's area, but with only 2.27 per cent of the population and two seats in the state assembly.[75] Inter-regional tensions as well as a fear of dominance of one region over the other was also manifested during the election of the Constituent Assembly in September–October, 1951. Seventy five Deputies were to be elected, of whom forty five were to represent Kashmir valley and Ladakh and thirty two for Jammu. The Praja Parishad filled upon nomination papers for only twenty nine constituencies in the Jammu province. Sixteen candidates of the Praja Parishad were eliminated at the nomination stage by rejecting their nomination papers on the ground of irregularity. Three days before the elections in Jammu, on October 12, 1951, the Praja Parishad announced boycott of the election, accusing state government of illegal practices and official interference in elections. In this situation, the Praja Parishad turned to other means to achieve its ends i.e. agitational politics. The Praja Parishad, a party founded by Balraj Madhok on the local organisational base of the Rastriya Swayamsevak Sangh (RSS) and strongly influenced by the Hindu nationalism, accused Sheikh Abdullah of trying to Islamize the administration, especially since he had broken up the Hindu majority district of Udhampur and was opposed to the rehabilitation of Hindu and Sikh refugees.[76]

The Praja Parishad openly came out to measure swords with the National Conference. To dramatize its opposition to Sheikh Mohammad Abdullah's administration, the Praja Parishad organised a campaign to demand total and unconditional integration of state with India. This campaign produced an atmosphere of tension which culminated in a major showdown between Praja Parishad and the state government.[77] In the third week of June 1952, the Praja Parishad leaders submitted a memorandum to the President of India. The memorandum claimed the rights of the people of Jammu province to determine their own future without interference from the National Conference and State Administration. The Praja Parishad sought to end Kashmiri domination over Jammu by demanding a complete integration of Jammu and Kashmir into the Union of India which would transfer power from the valley-based government to the central government.[78] In 1952, it began agitating for changes to this end with the support of the Bharatiya Jan Sangh, Hindu Mahasabha, Ram Rajya Parishad, Punjab Arya Samaj and some Akali leaders. The Parishad's Programme called for the abrogation of Article 370, full integration of the state with the union, full application of the Indian Constitution, removal of present distinction between the state subjects and Indian citizens, complete jurisdiction of the Supreme Court, removal of customs barriers between Kashmir and India, fresh elections to the Kashmir Constituent Assembly and investigation of corruption in the state administration by an impartial tribunal.[79] It questioned Sheikh Abdullah's motives by promoting to inconsistencies in his logic: "If Sheikh Abdullah hated Two Nation Theory, and his principles were the same as those of the Indian polity, there was the ground for not accepting full accession? Where was the need for a state constitution as distinct from a national constitution"? Jammu reverberated with the popular slogan "Ek Desh Mein Do Vidhan, Do Nishan, Do Pradhan, Nahni Chalega, Nahin Chalega" (in one country two constitutions, two flags and two chiefs will not work, will not be tolerated).[80] In the face of growing crisis, the Indian government summoned Sheikh Abdullah to New Delhi for consultation. Discussion between the two sides eventually resulted in the emergence of a significant development in the form of an agreement known as the Delhi Agreement that was finalised on July 24,1952. The provisions of Delhi Agreement which aimed at autonomy, for example, state flag, official language and Sadri-i-Riyasat (head of state) were immediately adopted by the Constituent Assembly and implemented by the state government. No further action was taken by the state government with regard to other provisions of the Delhi Agreement, particularly the transfer of the control of state telegraphs and telephone department and the extension of jurisdiction of the Supreme Court.[81] The Jammu people felt restive and Prem Nath Dogra the President of Praja Parishad party, on October 20, 1952, declared that they would start satyagrah in Jammu. The satyagrah assumed serious proportions. Meanwhile, the Jana Sangh party authorised its President Shyma Prasad Mukherjee, to approach the Indian government to redress the grievances of Jammu people, failing which he was to launch a movement in India in support of the Jammu agitation. He did so, but made little headway either with Jawaharlal Nehru Prime Minister of India or Sheikh Abdullah. His main request to Nehru was to exercise his influence on the Kashmir Premier so that, at least, the Delhi Agreement could be implemented in letter and spirit and to bring Kashmir into constitutional structure of free India.[82]

Consequently, on November 23, 1952, Praja Parishad started a prolonged Satyagrah with the main aim of getting Article 370 of the Indian Constitution deleted. The satyagrah assumed serious proportions. On February 2, 1953, state government announced the appointment of Janaki Nath Wazir Committee. Three questions referred to the Wazir Committee principally concerned with three categories of persons who were behind the agitation in Jammu. The state government under pressure had taken the initiative in appointing a committee to look into the economic aspect of the agitation.[83] Sheikh Mohammad Abdullah, in a broadcast from radio Kashmir Srinagar on April 17, 1953, said, "we have to provide equal opportunities to all sections of the people in accordance with the needs of each cultural unit in the state, appropriate provisions would be incorporated in the state's Constitution to ensure voluntary cooperation among various cultural groups in Jammu and Kashmir." The plan of Sheikh Abdullah, however, was not acceptable to the Dogras unless state would fully merge with Indian Union. Meanwhile, Shyam Prasad Mukherjee, in an attempt to strengthen the Praja Parishad agitation in Jammu, forced his entry into the territory of Jammu and Kashmir state without any ingress permit. He was arrested on May 11, 1953 and lodged in a sub-jail in Kashmir valley where he suddenly died on June 23, 1954. His death caused great uproar in Jammu and Praja Parishad laid the entire blame on state government.[84] The Prime Minister of India Jawaharlal Nehru, found the situation quit tense in Jammu and issued a statement on July 2, 1953 appealing the people of Jammu to withdraw their Satyagraha as the state government was considering grant of autonomy to its regions, particularly Jammu, while framing the constitution of the state. He also acted as an intermediate between the two groups and was able to arrange a compromise settlement. This phase ended with the dismissal and arrest of Sheikh Abdullah on August 8, 1953.[85]

The Praja Parishad felt that it had achieved a major success with the dismissal and arrest of Sheikh Abdullah and forgot about its demand for regional autonomy for Jammu region. Meanwhile, Bakshi Ghulam Mohammad, who succeeded Sheikh Abdullah, required the support of the people of Jammu to consolidate his political position. The state's constitution was given a final shape under the regime of Bakshi Ghulam Mohammad who over looked the commitment made by Sheikh Abdullah to guarantee provincial autonomy and set up regional council in Kashmir, Ladakh and Jammu. The people of Jammu, however, continued to complain against discriminatory treatment in services, the allotment of seats in professional colleges and allocation of development funds.[86] Prem Nath Dogra in his letter to Bakshi Ghulam Mohammad on Feb 4, 1954 reminded him of his assurance made to them and pleaded for their fulfillment. On April 1, 1954, Prem Nath Dogra in a memorandum against the constitutional proposals demanded the transfer of more and more power from Kashmir to the central government rather than demanding the sharing of political power with Kashmir. Bakshi Ghulam Mohammad, however, distributing favours to some of its leaders and thus tried to weaken the Praja Parishad movement.[87] Bakshi Ghulam Mohammad more or less served as a political stooge to the Central leadership of India to forward the latter's inexpedient and undemocratic designs of Jammu and Kashmir. It was during Bakshi's regime that the Presidential order of 1954 empowered the Indian Government to act on all matters in the Union List and not just defence, foreign affairs and communication. This was the beginning of erosion of autonomy for the state. Similarly, the Constitutional Amendment of 1958 brought the state under the control of the central administration, including extension of Articles 356 and 357 of the Indian constitution in 1964 to 1965. Article 249 was also made applicable to the state. The designations of Head of the State (Sadr-i-Riyasat) and Prime Minister were also changed to Governor and Chief Minister respectively. Furthermore, the Governor is to be appointed by the Centre rather than be a nominee of the elected State legislature. Thus, the inherent right of autonomy was snatched away from the state in a systematic but undemocratic way by the mid 1960's.

In November 1965, Karan Singh, the then Governor of the state, in a statement to London Times made a plea for dismemberment of the state through a linguistic reorganisation; Jammu joining Himachal Pradesh, the Kashmir Valley becoming a Kashmiri speaking state and Ladakh being centrally administered. It, however, reflected the expansion of Maharaja's domination and not the product of a natural evolution nor was it based on ethnic or linguistic consideration. Subsequently, in May 1967, in a joint letter to the then Prime Minister of India Indira Gandhi, seventy eight citizens of Jammu region made a demand for regional autonomy for Jammu within the framework of Jammu and Kashmir State. It stated that the acceptance of this stand would promote friendly relations between the principal regions and would make the politics of the state healthier and more secular. After the State Assembly Election of 1967, Chief Minister G.M. Sadiq and his government launched a massive attack on the movement of regional autonomy. To counter this agitation, the Jammu autonomy forum was setup. The meetings of the Jammu autonomy forum in Jammu, Udhampur, Kathua, Doda and Poonch were well attended and raised the demand for regional autonomy.[88] The Jammu autonomy forum sought a federal constitution to replace the unitary set up and revive the old idea of devolving power at the District, Block and Panchayat levels with safeguards for ethnic communities in each region.[89]

The simmering volcano in Jammu erupted again when four demonstrating students were killed in police firings on October 16 and 17, 1967, against the evil designs of shifting agricultural and Ayurvedic College to Srinagar. Initially, these colleges were to be established at Jammu.[90] Responding to the pressure, state government appointed Jammu and Kashmir Commission of Inquiry on November 6, 1967 popularly known as Gajendragadkar Commission. The Inquiry Commission's terms of reference included examination of policies regarding development, recruitment and admission to institution of higher education and considered generally the causes that led to irritations and tensions among regions of the state and to recommend remedial measures. The commission was required to suggest measures not only for equitable share of resources among the regions of the state but also for conveying a feeling of equal participation in the integrated development of the state.[91]

The Gajendragadkar Commission submitted its report to the state government in December1968. The Commission recommended certain radical changes in the composition of the state cabinet with political implications. The commission also suggested adoption of a convention of having Chief Minister from one region and Deputy Chief Minister from the other region. Other suggestions were to have equal number of cabinet ministers belonging to the Kashmir valley and Jammu region. Moreover, the commission recommended a full-fledged University for Srinagar and Jammu and provisions of law classes in Jammu University. A new Medical College was suggested and also a Regional Engineering College for Jammu if need arises. The Commission examined the regional composition of the state government employees as on April 1, 1967 and found that on this date, Jammu's share in the state services was only 36.1 per cent as against it having 44.2 per cent of the state population.[92]

All the recommendations of the commission were not accepted, particularly those which had political overtones. Subsequently, on February 18, 1970, the State Jana Sangh party started an agitation against the discriminatory and undemocratic policies of the state government. The demonstrators arrived at the secretariat in Jammu in the form of a procession and stopped Ministers and others who arrived to attend the office. Jana Sangh's demands included equal quantum of ration in Jammu and Srinagar, opening of a Medical College in Jammu and holding of civic elections. On February 22, 1970, the then Chief Minister of the State G. M. Sadiq arranged a meeting with the Jana Sangh representatives led by Prem Nath Bazaz in a bid to persuade the Jana Sangh to call off the agitation.[93] The State Government, accordingly, setup a Commission of Inquiry also known as Sikri Commission on June 2, 1979. The main task of Inquiry Commission was to examine the question of imbalances among three regions of the State. The term of reference related to development programmes and politics recruitment to services and admission in the institutions of higher learning. The Sikri Commission submitted its report in August 1980. So far as the admission to professional institutions and grant of scholarship and loans were concerned, the Commission had suggested some improvement in the prevailing procedures to ensure the selection of meritorious students for educational facilities. So far as recruitment policies were concerned, the commission found that in Gazetted services Jammu had 13 per cent less share and in non-gazette services 7 per cent less share and Kashmir had an excess of 12 per cent in Gazetted, 8 per cent in Non-Gazetted and 5 per cent in class fourth services. The commission also found imbalances in financial expenditure and development programmes at regional levels.[94]

However, these recommendations were not implemented and in consequence the people of Jammu started another agitation known as Durbar Move Agitation. The Government's bid to rationalise the century old Durbar Move again kicked up regional passion in Jammu region. The people of Jammu region protested against this order describing it as part of conspiracy to divide the state between two regions of Jammu and Kashmir. They maintained that the making of two regions of the state was through Durbar Move. They charged that "Government's decision was blatant discrimination against the people of Jammu region and reflective of perpetuating Kashmiri domination over the people of Jammu". The Bar Association of Jammu also condemned the government's decision in strongest words and called one day protest strike by lawyers on October 9, 1987. The Bar Association started indefinite bandh from November 7, 1987.[95]

Subsequently, on November 14, 1987, the state government withdrew its order of October 7, 1987. The Bar Association of Jammu called off its 37 days agitation on the same day. Again, Jammu Mukti Morcha was launched on March 2, 1990 to achieve the objective of forming a separate Jammu State. The leaders of Mukti Morcha believed that with the backing of the central government, the Kashmiri rulers had always manipulated their permanent dominating positions in all walks of life and thus denied Jammu its due share in political power and economic development. They have come to the conclusion as according to the leaders of Mukti Morcha, "no half way measures like Regional Development Boards, Regional Autonomy, the Jammu sub-state within the framework of the state of Jammu and Kashmir, can provide a durable solution". Thus, they believe that the only remedy of inter-regional relations of the state is its trifurcation.[96]

Meanwhile, the state government had constituted a Regional Autonomy Committee on November 29, 1996 to recommend ways and means for granting Regional Autonomy to the three regions of the state. On April 13, 1999 the Regional Autonomy Committee submitted its report to the state government. The report recommended two models for regional autonomy. While recommending reconstitution of regions it had stated that regional or provincial councils should be set up to meet the requirements of devolution of powers to different regions in the state.

The second model suggested by it was that the devolution of powers to people could be ensured through establishment of District Councils.[97] The people of Jammu alleged that reconstitution of province or region recommended for Jammu division was bound to promote communal divide. Moreover, the citizen forum constituted a conglomerate of various social and political organisations of Jammu also rejected the recommendations of regional autonomy committee on May 23, 2000 and threatened to launch state wide agitations against it. They called the report of regional autonomy committee as an attempt by the National Conference to disintegrate the state from the union of India and divide it on communal lines.[98]

Meanwhile, several political, social and student organisations of Jammu province gave a call for bandh on June 29, 2000, against the adoption of motion seeking grant of greater autonomy by the state legislature. The leaders demanded the trifurcation of the state so that Ladakh was converted into a Union Territory Status and Jammu being treated as a separate State.[99] In May 2001, when K.C. Pant, the Chief negotiator of the Government of India appointed to negotiate with the political parties of the state, visited Jammu and the people of the region again reiterated their demand for a separate statehood for Jammu province. Also, on July 14, 2001, when the President of Pakistan General Pervez Musharaf visited India to discuss the 'Kashmir issue' at Agra summit; the Jammu based radical Hindu leaders of Bhartiya Janta Party gave a call for Jammu bandh to launch their protest against solving the problem as per wishes of the people of Kashmir.[100]

Ladakhi Identity and Regional Consciousness

Ladakh is geographically, ethnically and culturally unique part of India. Situated beyond the Himalayas, it has around 236,539 population which inhabits an area of 96,000 sq. km against 19,000 sq. km of Kashmir and 26,000 sq. km of Jammu i.e., more than double than the rest of the state. It has 800 miles of common border with China- 350 miles with Tibet and 450 miles with Sinkang (census 2001).[101] Separated from the rest of the country and the world by Zojila pass that is 11,530 feet above sea level, the region is further sub-divided by Fatu La, 13,400 feet above sea level and was divided into two districts of Leh and Kargil in 1979. The Buddhists are nearly more than half of the population of the region (52 per cent) and mainly concentrated in Leh district while the rest are Muslims (48 per cent) who mostly belong to Shia sect and live in Kargil district. Ladakhi, also called Bodhi, Balti, Dardi and Shina are the main languages spoken in the region (census 2001). Urdu is being spoken as the second language because as their mother tongue is Ladakhi.[102] The people of the region have their historical, racial, lingual, cultural, religious and commercial ties with the surrounding regions of Tibet and Northern Himachal Pradesh. The belief system, customs, traditions, food pattern, dress pattern, architecture, indigenous system of medicine, fine arts and literature of the region has its origin in Tibet and its neighbouring territories.[103] The Ladakh region was a Buddhist kingdom conquered by the Dogra General Zorawar Singh in 1834 and since then, it continues to be a part of Jammu and Kashmir state much like the Jammu region.[104]

The people of Ladakh, after independence, did not like the idea of following the Kashmir valley leaders who held the view that they were entitled to rule entire state on the basis of nullity (emptiness) of the treaty of Amritsar. The Ladakhi's held the view that nullity should not affect them at all. The Ladakhis also did not see any future for them in Kashmir if it went over to Pakistan. Thus, they decided to cut themselves off from the state and throw their lot with India for their future hopes.[105] Accordingly, on May 14, 1949, the President of Buddhist Association Chhewang Rigzin, submitted a memorandum to the then Prime Minister of India in which he stated that "we have the right to determine our own future apart from other communities and people inhabiting the state and that we cannot be affected by the result of the forthcoming plebiscite in the event of its being favourable to Pakistan. We are a separate nation by all tests - race, language, religion, culture-determining nationality, the only link connecting us with the other people of the state being the bond of a common ruler".[106]

Simultaneously, the leadership from Ladakh started its demand for special status for Ladakh. In March 1952, Kushak Bakula submitted a memorandum to Sheikh Abdullah in which he urged that a separate Legislative Assembly of fifteen members, with an Executive Council responsible to it, should be set up for Ladakh to run the internal administration of the Ladakh region.[107] Ladakh would largely bear the same relationship to Jammu and Kashmir State as the latter does to India, with the local legislature as the only authority competent to make laws for the region of Ladakh and to control administration.

In this memorandum, Kushak Bakula said that Ladakh would have little or no voice in the state's seventy five member Constituent Assembly of the State of Jammu and Kashmir, where they were in point of race, language and culture perfect strangers to the rest of the members. In September 1952, a resolution was passed at the Ladakh Tehsil National Conference held a meeting under the Chairmanship of Kushak Bakula stating that, "Ladakh's relationship with Kashmir would last as long as the state's accession to India endures and that the inhabitants of Ladakh should be allowed to manage their own affairs." By another resolution, it demanded setting up of five members' elected statutory advisory committee to supervise internal administration and that no measure concerning Ladakh tehsils political, economic, and social and religious life should be adopted by the state government without the proposed Advisory Committee previous approval.[108]

After the dismissal of Sheikh Abdullah in 1953, Ladakhi's hoped that his successor Bakshi Gulam Mohammad would do all out to satisfy their political, economic and cultural needs. Kushak Bakula lost no time in meeting Bakshi Ghulam Mohammad and submitted to him a memorandum containing concrete suggestions for improvement of educational, economic and social conditions of the people of Ladakh. Among other things, opening of more educational institutions and granting scholarship to Ladakhi students for technical and professional training in India were also demanded. The memorandum also urged that Bodhi language be made the medium of instruction in primary classes and it shall be given the same status as Sanskrit and Arabic in University curriculum.[109]

As a result of the demand raised by Ladakhis, the state government initiated steps to reorient its Ladakh policy. In November 1953, Kushak Bakula was inducted into the State's Council of Minister as a Deputy Minister in charge of Ladakh affairs. The controversy aroused over the powers and functions of Deputy Minister of Ladakh affairs as these were not defined. Kushak Bakula, therefore, offered to step down if it was not invested with powers over the administration of Ladakh. The government immediately realised the gravity of the situation and conceded some powers to him with regard to the matters pertaining to Ladakh. Meanwhile, the Government of India with a view to strengthening the administration of the Ladakh region, proposed an administrative set-up which was used largely on the philosophy and experience of the North Eastern Frontier Administration. The state government, however, was not in favour of the North Eastern Frontier type administrative experiment in Ladakh which had the whole hearted support of the Ladakhis.[110] The state government did away with it on the plea that Ladakh was an integral part of the Jammu and Kashmir state and should therefore, be administered on the pattern followed in other parts of the state. The Ladakhi leadership was not happy with the idea of the state government. Towards the end of 1964, Kushak Bakula called on Lal Bhadur Shastri, the then Prime Minister of India, in New Delhi and apprised him of the situation in Ladakh. He told the Prime Minister about the absence of rule of law in Ladakh and imposition of unsympathetic officials from the Kashmir valley on the Ladakh region.[111]

The state government, at the behest of the central government, appointed a ten member high power committee known as Ladakh Development Committee to advise it in regard to the policies and issues affecting good governance and speedy development of Ladakh. Kushak Bakula, by virtue of being the Minister of State for Ladakh Affairs, was to function as its Chairman and Agaha Ibrahim Shah, member of Legislative Council from Kargil, as its Vice President. But the people of Ladakh were not satisfied with the steps taken by the state government. Sonam Wangyal voiced the unhappiness of the Ladakhis at a press conference in New Delhi on April 16, 1965.

While complaining that the state government did not take enough interest in Ladakh's development, he demanded an enquiry by a central government team into the causes of stagnation in Ladakh. The people of Ladakh continued to be unhappy with the state government and its policy towards Ladakh which evidently, was one of the neglect and apathy. Kushak Bakula who was elected as Member of Parliament from Ladakh in 1967 election also expressed resentment at Ladakh's slow pace of development. He alleged that the development of Ladakh was neglected and central grants for scheme to develop it had remained largely unutilised by state government. He also alleged that there was no reservation for the people of Ladakh in the state services. In August 1967, Kushak Bakula submitted a memorandum to the Prime Minister of India in which he demanded the separation of Ladakh from the State of Jammu and Kashmir, a North Eastern Frontier (NEFA) type of administration for Ladakh and no middle man rule of the state government in dealing with central finances meant for Ladakh. He urged that central assistance could come directly to Ladakh through Governor rather than the state secretariat.[112]

The pleading committee of Ladakh Congress had also submitted a memorandum to Gajendragadkar Commission in April 1967. The memorandum alleged that the rights of Ladakhis have been violated and their genuine demands were ignored by the state government. The Commission, however, recommended that there should be a full-fledged Cabinet Minister belonging to Ladakh. Besides other recommendations, the Commission recommended that there should be Statutory Regional Development Board and also District Recruitment Board for Ladakh.[113]

The reaction of the people of Ladakh towards the Inquiry Commission was favourable. They felt that their voice had found due expression in the Commission's Report. Kushak Bakula started enlisting support of some members of Indian parliament and important functionaries of the Government of India for building pressure for a speedy implementation of the Commission's recommendation and recognising Ladakh as a separate political and constitutional entity. The State government sent Peer Giyas-uddin, who was the Minister of Ladakh Affairs, to Leh, on April 29, 1969 to hold discussions with the Buddhist Action Committee regarding its demands. An agreement was reached between the Buddhist Action Committee's Chairman Koshak Togdam and Peer Giyas-uddin.[114] As a result of the agreement, the agitation was called off over, connected with property dispute, at the instance of Kushak Bakula and Sonam Wangyal on June 11, 1969. However, the demands of the Buddhist were not conceded. Subsequently, in July, 1969, Kushak Bakula again met the then Prime Minister of India Indira Gandhi, at Delhi to request her to consider the demand for NEFA type administration in Ladakh in view of the Chief Minister's dilatory tactics on the question of implementation of the recommendations of the Gajendragadkar Commission. During her visit to Kashmir in August 1969, Mrs. Indira Gandhi was reported to have made a passing reference, during her meeting with chief minister, to Kushak Bakula's anxiety for the recommendation of the Commission which ensured the maintenance of integrity of the state.[115]

Subsequently, the people of Ladakh threatened that if their legitimate demands were not fulfilled, they would resort to agitational means. In the face of the threat of an agitation in Ladakh, the then Chief Minister of the state Syed Mir Qasim, undertook a tour to Leh in September 1973. During his visit, the Chief Minister was called upon by various deputationists whom he assured that his Government would look into their problems and grievances. But nothing concrete came out.[116] On September 13, 1974, Kushak Bakula again demanded that Ladakh should be made union territory. He said that region should be declared as Scheduled Tribes Area and its people as Scheduled Tribe as had been done in case of other Himalayan regions. He urged for setting up of a Development Council which would function both as an administrative body and legislative organ for Ladakh district. He also demanded that two colleges should be established in Ladakh, one in Leh and another at Kargil.[117]

Sheikh Mohammad Abdullah was installed as Chief Minister of the state on Feb. 25, 1975, as a result of Indira-Sheikh Accord. In view of the earlier bitterness, Sheikh Abdullah was keen to win over the people of Ladakh to seek their cooperation in the working of the government. Ladakh was opened to tourist traffic for the first time in 1975. This ancient land of Ladakh has turned to be one of the main attractions to foreign tourists. Development activities in Ladakh during the first four years had changed the economy of the region. The people of Ladakh carefully watched the interest which the state government evidenced towards their economic, educational, social and cultural advancement.[118] Meanwhile, some Muslim leaders of Kargil had a grievance against the State Government that only a representative of Leh sub-division Buddhist was taken in the State Ministry and Kargil was ignored totally. They demanded that Kargil should be made separate district and not treated as a subdivision of Ladakh district. As a consequence, on July 1, 1979, the state government bi-furcated the Ladakh district into two separate districts of Leh and Kargil. The people of Leh felt that Kargil was being given better treatment at the cost of Leh district and as such their relations with state government started deteriorating day after day.[119]

The Ladakh Buddhist Association in early 1980 carried out a movement demanding allocation of land to the Tibetan refugees in Ladakh. This resulted in sharp polarisation of Ladakh along communal lines, with Shia majority Kargil joining hands with the Kashmiris. The "Greater Kashmir" idea influenced the polity in Ladakh throughout

1980's and 1990's that effectively divided the sentiments of the people of Kargil and also created confusion and a gulf between Kargil and Ladakh. The artificial division along communal lines is still being used as an argument to quell any strong voice from Ladakh in the current discourse on the Kashmir issue.[120]

After Sheikh Abdullah's death, when Farooq Abdullah became the Chief Minister on September 8, 1982, the people of Ladakh hoped that the new government would honour the previous government's commitment regarding the grant of Scheduled Tribe status. The state cabinet headed by Farooq Abdullah visited Ladakh on October 12, 1982. The discussion with the Action Committee among other things covered its two demands namely, conferment of Tribal Status on Ladakh and grant of autonomy to them regarding economic and financial matters. It was agreed that the Chief Minister and the leaders of Ladakh action committee would meet the Prime Minister of India jointly to hammer out an agreed solution to the vexed problem.[121]

The proposed meeting with the Rajiv Gandhi, the then Prime Minister, did not materialise for one reason or the other and the people started getting restive and frustrated again. However, to press its demand, the Ladakh Action Committee deputed four member delegation headed by Sonam Wangyal to Jammu for discussions with the authorities on Jan 29, 1983. The delegation had two sittings with the then Planning Commissioner Ashok Jaitely, and other officials that were concerned with the development of Ladakh. The delegations also had a meeting with Chief Minister Farooq Abdullah who assured them that the State Government had recommended to the central government that Ladakh should be granted Scheduled Tribe Status. In April, 1983, the central government clarified that the actual implementation of the decision to grant Scheduled Tribe Status depended upon the state government under Article 370 of the Indian constitution.[122]

Farooq Abdullah on July 19, 1983, however, expressed his inability to grant Scheduled Tribe Status to the people of Ladakh region. The State Government's decision was causing fresh unrest in Ladakh region. On July 21, 1983, Kushak Bakula and P. Nangayal, Member of Parliament from Leh criticized the Chief Minister for denying Scheduled Tribe Status to the people of Ladakh. They said chief minister was trying to mislead the people by suggesting that the decision announced by the Central government was only related to the people of Leh district and not the entire region of Ladakh. However, the induction of Ghulam Mohammad Shah as Chief Minister on July 2, 1984, brought a wave of jubilation in Ladakh where the people entertained fresh hopes regarding the redressal of their grievances and fulfillment of pending demands.[123] The meeting was held on August 28, 1984, between the Ladakh Action Committee and Chief Minister and other ministers. In the meeting, the Chief Minister himself raised the issue of granting of Scheduled Tribe Status to all Ladakhis. Unfortunately, despite hectic deliberations, the matter could not be finalised during the Action Committee's stay in Srinagar. However, another delegation from Ladakh which among other, included Sonam Wangyal, called on the Chief Minister on Jan. 25, 1985 at Jammu. The delegation expressed unhappiness at the delay regarding the granting of Scheduled Tribe Status to the Ladakh region. The State Government, however, made the necessary recommendation under Article 342 of the Constitution of India. Initially, this even pawed the way for conferment of Tribe Status on eight selected Ladakhi ethnic groups identified by the Registrar General of India on the basis of mini-census conducted by him for this purpose.[124]

On October 7, 1989, the Central government accorded Scheduled Tribe Status to eight tribal communities. The eight tribal communities are Balti, Beda, Bolo, Brokpa, Drokpa, Changpa, Gara-Mon and Puringpa.[125] The Ladakh Buddhist Association has now changed their demand from Tribal Status to Union Territory Status. The trouble began with a minor scuffle between a Buddhist and some Muslim youth in Leh market in July 1989 which then snowballed into a violent separatist struggle by the Ladakh Buddhist Association. Its members demanded that Ladakh be given separate constitutional status as a union territory. The members of Ladakh Buddhist Association accused the Kashmir Sunni Muslims of inciting the local Argon Muslims who were unequivocally in the minority and were dictating terms to the Buddhist majority and thereby dominate both the administration and economy. Buddhists also complained that the rich Bodhi language was being suppressed in favour of Urdu, now being imposed on Ladakhi children.[126]

Subsequently, in February 1991, the Ladakhis gathered in a rally in Leh demanding an end to Kashmir domination. The Ladakh Buddhist Association leaders in rally declared that they could settle for nothing less than Union Territory Status for Ladakh. In August 1991, the Ladakh Buddhist Association called a bandh in Ladakh and took to direct confrontation with the Government of India to free Ladakh from Kashmir. In October 1991, the Ladakh Buddhist Association threatened to resume the agitation as the central and state government had failed to implement the October 29, 1989 agreement which had promised Autonomous Hill Council for Ladakh. The State Government sent an urgent signal on October 31, 1991 to district administration in Leh to urge the Ladakh Buddhist Association to defer its proposed agitation from November 3, 1991 for Union Territory Status to Ladakh. The Ladakh Buddhist Association agreed to hold discussion with the government and postponed its proposed agitation from November 3, following assurance by the State Government that their demand be accorded top priority.[127]

On November 19, 1991, a meeting was held in Jammu between the Ladakh Buddhist Association and Governor of Jammu and Kashmir Girish Chander Sexana. The Ladakh Buddhist Association reiterated its demand for adequate safeguard for the identity and aspirations of the people of Ladakh, adding that it sought a framework wherein the elected representative of the people would have an effective say and involvement in all matter pertaining to Ladakh region. They also demanded the application of the Sixth Schedule[128] of the Constitution of India to Ladakh region. The Governor assured them that the State Government was aware of the difficulties faced by the people of the region. The government indicated its decision to formulate other options which along with Ladakh Buddhist Association's demand for an Autonomous Hill District Council for Ladakh would be considered at the next round of discussion in January 1992.[129] Meanwhile, the Union Home Minister S.B. Chavan also had a meeting with a delegation of the Ladakh Buddhist Association on April 8, 1992. The Ladakh Buddhist Association reportedly claimed that modalities for setting up the Autonomous District Hill Development Council had been worked out with the State government; therefore, the follow up measures would be taken without any further delay.[130] The Union Home Minister responded by saying that a bill for Autonomous Council would be introduced in the session of the parliament if the Ladakh Buddhist Association claim was found correct. The Ladakh Buddhist Association demanded the application of all provisions under Schedule Five and

Six of the Indian Constitution to Leh District as applied to North-Eastern States. They also demanded the status of a Cabinet Minister for the chairman of the proposed council and of a full-fledged secretary for its executive officer. The Union Home Minister fixed May 20, 1992 for the next round of talk.[131]

The leaders of the Ladakh Buddhist Association were determined to get a share in political power in the state and announced that they would revive their stir for their original demand of Union Territory Status if no decision was taken on granting them the Autonomous Hill Council. In obvious bid to build pressure on the Central Government, Ladakh Buddhist Association organised a massive rally on May 11, 1992 in Leh and other parts of district.[132] For the first time in recent years, the Head Lamas of the three monasteries-Finang, Thicksay and Stakna, joined the agitation by taking out procession at Leh on May 12, 1992 but the discussions were again inclusive. Subsequently, a meeting was held in Jammu on February 10, 1993, between the representative of Ladakh Buddhist Association and State government. An agreement was reached on the composition including members of the General Council and the Executive Committee of the proposed Autonomous Hill Council.[133]

In October, 1993, the Union Home Minister S. B. Chavan, promised to introduce a bill in the parliament to grant an Autonomous Hill Council for the Ladakh region. However, the central government used to introduce the bill causing great resentment among the people of Leh district.[134] Meanwhile, the coordination committee of Ladakh Autonomous Hill Council gave a call for bandh in August, 1994 to press the central government to introduce a bill in the parliament. In response, the people of Ladakh observed a total bandh on August 25 and boycotted the Ladakh festival inauguration on August 28, 1994, by the Union Ministers for Tourism and Civil Aviation Ghulam Nabi Azad. When the central government ignored the demands of Ladakhis to introduce a bill in parliament, the coordination committee gave a call for 24 hours bandh call from March 18, 1995. During bandh normal life was completely thrown out of gear. To force the Central Government to fulfill its demand for setting up an Autonomous Hill Council, the coordination committee announced launching of a relay dharna from March 20, 1995. The committee also decided to intensify their struggle till the central government orders constitution of an Autonomous Hill

Council.[135] Therefore, in order to overcome the Ladakhis Agitation, the central government at last enacted the Ladakh Autonomous Hill Development Council (LAHDC) Act in May, 1995. This Act consists of ten chapters and describe in detail regarding the constitution of Ladakh Autonomous Hill Development Council, its territorial constituencies, election to the council, oath of affirmation by members etc. In the first two chapters, the total number of seats in the LAHDC elected on the basis of adult franchise will be twenty six. The Governor has been empowered to nominate four members to the Council from among the principal minority and women in the district to the members of the Council. Third chapter is related with the powers and functions of the Council while fourth deals with conduct of the business of the Council. Chapter fifth deals with the Executive Council, its composition, powers and functions etc. Chapter sixth deals with the officers and servants of the Council including Chief Executive officer and Secretary. Chapter seven is related with the transfer of land to the council while the eighth chapter deals with the funds and audit of the council. Chapter ninth deals the constitution of inter-district advisory council and chapter tenth deals with the miscellaneous power of council, power to issue direction, dissolution of the council, power to make rules and regulations.[136]

The elections of Leh Autonomous Hill Development Council were held in August 1999. The Congress (I) won 24 seats and independent only two. The Leh Autonomous Hill Development Council (LAHDC) was functioning smoothly, but after the formation of the National Conference government in 1996 the ministers reportedly started interfering with the function of the Leh Autonomous Hill Development Council (LAHDC). On February 12, 1997, the Chief Executive Councillor, Thupstan Chhewang, said that, "there were some short-comings in the LAHDC Act, so the Act ought to be reviewed.[137] After the review, the Act should be suitably amended in the interest of the people of Ladakh region". He further said that "the employees of state government in the district had to stick to dual loyalty because although the loyalty of these was transferred to the LAHDC, they had to depend on the State Government as far as their promotional avenues and mobility within the state is concerned". All these factors had resulted in blunting the effectiveness of the functioning of the Ladakh Autonomous Hill Development Council (LAHDC).[138]

The Ladakh Buddhist Association alleged on March 15, 1997 that all possible efforts were made to undermine the LAHDC by the State government. In a letter to Chief Minister Farooq Abdullah, the President of Ladakh Buddhist association Tsering Narbee Lampa, said the popular demand of conferring Cabinet Minister' status to the Chief Executive Councillor was turned down by the state government. He said as against rightful due of rupees eighty nine crore, the Leh district was given a mere rupees 24 crore as plan allocation for 1996-97.[139] The Ladakh Buddhist Association demanded the reservation in jobs and in other sphere of development as well. In June, 2000 alarmed by the State Autonomy Report seeking restoration of the pre-1953 position in Jammu and Kashmir, the people of Ladakh region favoured either trifurcation of the state or a grant of Union Territory Status. The Ladakh Buddhist Association felt the State Autonomy Committee Report, if implemented would undermine the existence of Ladakh as a distinctive ethno-cultural identity. The President of Ladakh Buddhist Association, Tesering Samphel said, "any political arrangement should take into account the aspirations of the people of Ladakh region. They should also be granted maximum internal autonomy".[140]

On June 19, 2000 a large number of Ladakhis and several political parties, launched a week long protest and demanded Union Territory Status for the Ladakh region against the Jammu and Kashmir's move for greater autonomy to the state. The President of Ladakh Buddhist Association Tesering Samphel, cautioned the Centre and State governments that if the present trend continued, Ladakhi Buddhists would not hesitate to knock the doors of United Nations and seek mass asylum in any other country. He strongly opposed the State Autonomy Committee Report and announced his support to the cause of Union Territory Status.[141] Ladakhis have also joined hands with Jammuties on the issue of reorganisation of state, a movement headed by All Parties Jammu Nationalist Front (APJNF) asking for trifurcation of the state. Simultaneously, the Ladakh Buddhist Association holds a rally at Leh on November 19, 2001, to demonstrate their desire for declaring Ladakh as a Union Territory Status. Meanwhile a delegation of LAHDC led by its Chief Councillor Thupstan Chhewang, had gone to Delhi to meet national leaders stressing the need for creating a separate Ministry on the pattern of the North-East to look after the affairs of Ladakh. Again, the movement for separation of Ladakh from Jammu and

Kashmir State and the creation of a Union Territory Status reached an all-time high in 2002 when Leh units of all political parties were unanimously dissolved and local leadership cutting across the ideological and party affiliation formed the Ladakh Union Territory Front. The Ladakh Union Territory Front candidates won Assembly Elections unopposed and uncontested as there was complete unanimity for the creation of Union Territory Status. This voice is seen still in the anal of Ladakh.[142]

Sub-Regional Identities in Jammu and Kashmir

Every pluralistic society comprises many religious and ethno-linguistic minority groups. They may be landless nomadic communities, migrants, indigenous racial entities or others. The major peculiarity of minorities is that they are different in ethnographical characteristics, cultural legacy, economic condition or racial makeup from that of majority in a particular area, state or region.[143] Despite the fact that identity of the state started taking shape during colonial period in Jammu and Kashmir, a Muslim majority State ruled by Hindu Dogra Maharaja Hari Singh, the religion could not become the password of its identity. Rather the oppressive rule of the king had created a conducive environment for blurring the boundaries among the different religious, ethnic and linguistic communities in the state and thereby constructed the secular and plural identity of the state. Neither religion nor ethnicity was given much space in the politics of Jammu and Kashmir, despite this fact that there was potential for communal and ethnic conflict.[144] The identity of the state at that time was neither communal nor ethnic. It was secular, multilayered, plural, open and flexible. Over the years, the logic of majority-minority politics has percolate to the sub-regional level. Each region in the state has a plural socio-cultural makeup and its heterogeneity has allowed several alternatives to the populace for building a political majority along the linguistic, religious, regional, cultural and caste lines. The Jammu region witnessed growing assertion of Gujjar and Pahari identities. In Ladakh, Zanaskar's Buddhist minority (part of Kargil district) started asserting its identity independent of Kargil's Muslim–majority populace.[145]

Jammu: Gujjars, Paharis, Dogras

Gujjars are the third largest community in Jammu and Kashmir; they are partially nomadic and mostly Muslims. They are divided into three groups: nomads (20 per cent), settled (30 per cent) and semi-nomads (50 per cent) who live on the fringes of the plains in the winter and climb up to the high pastures in the summer. They are called Basneeks. The nomads are divided into Baniharas[146] and Bakerwalas.[147] The Bakkarwal Gujjars are further divided into the Kahnaris and Ilias. The language of Gujjars popularly called Gojri was termed Parimu or Hindki by Walter Lawrence.[148] It was categorised as Rajisthani in the census conducted before partition. The linguist George Grierson argued that Gojri was the second major language after Kashmiri in the state. However, Gojri is not recognised in the state constitution.[149]

Gujjars are present in the entire state except Leh and Kargil. In the Kashmir division, the concentration of the Gujjars is on the mountain slopes and side valleys in the areas of Kokernag, Kangan, Tral, Doru, Phalgam, Shopian, Kulgam, Handwara, Karnah, Kupwara and Uri tehsils. In Jammu region, the Gujjars dominate in the border districts of the Rajouri and Poonch, particularly the tehsils pockets found in Baderwah, Doda, Gool, Kishtiwar, Kathua and Udhampur areas. Gujjars constituted 9 per cent of state's population (census 1981).[150] From 1961 to 1981, the census was conducted on a linguistic basis and owing to the electoral arithmetic in the state; Gujjars were split into various linguistic groups –Hindu, Rajisthani, Punjabi, Gojri, Bakerwali, Pahari, Parimu and Urdu. Also, the bilingual Gujjars living in the areas dominated by Kashmiri and Dogri speakers were assimilated into these linguistic groups.[151] Most Gujjar leaders, therefore, simply reject the census figures. They estimated the current strength of Gujjars to be 10 to 15 lakh based on the share of 4.31 lakh in 1931[152] or from their own census conducted informally at district, village and Panchayat levels in 1998.[153]

The Gujjars first gained political prominence when Sheikh Abdullah was trying to rope in the Muslim-majority districts of Rajouri and Poonch and the Kashmiri-speaking Muslims of the Doda into "Greater Kashmir" in the late1970's. Mrs. Indira Gandhi devised a new electoral arithmetic which calculated that the Dogras and Gujjars together were numerically more than the Kashmiris. Thus, she cultivated the Gujjars as a counter weight to the Kashmiri Muslims. A conscious decision seems to have been taken to arouse the ethnic Gujjars as opposed to the religious Muslim consciousness of their community.[154]

Initially, the Gujjar identity was promoted through culture, music, literature, and art. Besides it, radio programmes and the state cultural academy also played their part in this respect. It was in 1975 when Jammu Radio Station started Gojri broadcasts at Jammu, Kathua and Poonch along with fortnightly programmes on Doordarshan that boosted the morale of Gojri speakers and writers. Some private institutions and organisations included Anjuman Taraqqi, Gujri Adab with district level branches, Adabi Sangat Kashmir, Idara Adbiyat, Gojri Adabi board, besides dramatic and cultural clubs were involved in promoting Gojri language and literature. Gojri journals and magazines such as Al- Insan, Nawai Qoum, Gujjar Desh and Gujjar Gunj, published from Jammu focused on political and economic issues affecting the community. The recent publication of the monthly magazine Awaz-e-Gujar and establishment of a Gojri library and the Gojjri research institute started by the Gujjar Desh Charitable Trust is another important step in this direction. The Gojri section of the Jammu and Kashmir academy of Art, Culture and Languages started in 1987 also played an important role by preserving Gojri Folk culture giving recognition and support to Gojri writers, publications of a comprehensive Gojri dictionary and Sheeraza- a quarterly with poems, songs, short stories and research papers on the Gujjars.[155] In 1975, Gujjar and Bakkarwal welfare board was constituted and funds for welfare schemes were earmarked in five-year plans. Promotion of education by opening mobile schools, scholarship schemes and building hostels in Rajouri and Poonch gave birth to new literate strata in Gujjar society. Being a third largest linguistic group of the state after Kashmiri and Dogri, the Gujjars are losing their identity as tribe gradually because they are not getting the opportunity to work on their identity. Unfortunately, there is a kind of stigma attached to the word "Gujjar" in the Kashmiri society. For tribals, this is considered as an offending act. With this type of relation between Gujjars and Kashmiris, a wedge is getting created between larger Muslim societies of Kashmir.[156] The recent public mobilisation over the Amarnath land issue in August 2008 in the state saw Gujjars isolated in both the regions. In Jammu, they are being targeted by extremist Hindu Rightwing as Muslim minority setting up dozens of Gujjar houses in Jammu, Samba and Kathua districts of Jammu region. Similarly in Kashmir valley, some slogans although aimed at Ghulam Nabi Azad, contained intemperate remarks about Gujjars.[157]

In order to express themselves fully and save the community from getting marginalised, Gujjars of Jammu and Kashmir need to be considered as ethnolinguistic minority and their rights established accordingly. Gujjars, being a nomadic tribe, deserve safeguards and other privileges under the Constitution of India as a Schedule Tribe. Articles 15, 16 and 17 of the Indian constitution guarantee the right to equality as the fundamental right. Under cultural and educational rights Article 29 protect the interest of the minorities including their language and culture.[158]

Pahari Identity

Pahari community lives on both sides of the line of control (LOC) in Rajouri and Poonch districts of Jammu region as well as Kupwara district and parts of Baramulla and Anantnag districts of Kashmir region. Though, it has equally proud heritage, the urge for identity became sharper after Gujjars acquired a Schedule Tribe status. They speak dialects of Poonchi, Mirpuri and Mazaffarabadi and have come together under the umbrella term Pahari to claim a Schedule Tribe status and share in political and economic power. Pahari's include the followers of Islam and Hinduism.

As a result, new renaissance movement of Paharis, a standardised language is being evolved in which unwritten literature is being written. Historically, the Pahari speaking areas lies on the route through which most of the cultural currents from the rest of the country passed enroute to Kashmir. It has still proud records which are being revived of its past heroes, political leaders, Buddhist Monks, Hindu saints, Muslim Sufis, warriors and literary personalities.[159]

Pahari consciousness started gaining ground in 1970's to counter the impression that there were only three large communities in the state: Kashmiris, Dogras and Gujjars. The central government was cultivating the Gujjars and the Paharis felt neglected. Since their immediate political competition was with the Gujjars, the leadership sought to weave a Pahari identity centered on its language that distinguished them from the Gujjars. The Jammu and Kashmir Pahari cultural forum established in 1969 was essentially a reaction to the Gujjar welfare forum. In 1977, the Paharis demanded a welfare board and in 1983-84 they sought Schedule Tribe status. Some Pahari speaking areas in Himachal Pradesh already enjoy this status.[160]

In 1989, Farooq Abdullah accepted the demand of a welfare board but it was not implemented. Jammu and Kashmir Governor G. C. Sexana and his successor Governor Krishna Rao supported the Pahari's demand and recommended to the central government to grant them Scheduled Tribe status. This has not been accepted till date.[161]

More recently, Pahari leaders have been demanding the creation of new Pahari region, separating predominantly Muslims of Rajouri-Poonch from Jammu division with an Autonomous Hill Council (AHC) on the pattern of Leh Autonomous Hill Council. The nature of grievances is familiar in terms of under development and backwardness of districts, dominance of Jammu district in the share of civil services, public sector undertakings and other important institutions.[162] The Pahari leaders argue that "the region has a distinct geography, history, language, culture as well as socio-economic conditions". Comparing the per capita expenditure in Rajouri and Poonch with Leh and Kargil, they argue that "if Leh could have an autonomous hill council why not us"?[163]

Another demand for setting up an Autonomous Hill Council has been put forward by the Chenab valley region consisting of Doda district, tehsils like Gool-Gulabgarh, Doda, Basangarh of Udhampur district and Lohai and Bani of Kathua district with scheduled tribe status. The proponents of this demand divide Jammu and Kashmir State into four natural regions. (a) sub-mountainous and semi-mountainous tract or plain areas of Udhampur and Kathua districts (b) outer hill region including the districts of Doda, Rajouri, Poonch and the hilly areas of the districts of Udhampur and Kathua; (c) the Jhelum valley region which means the entire Kashmir valley and (d) the Tibetan and semi-Tibetan tracts including Ladakh and Gilgit. It is argued that since the Chenab valley region is a distinct and independent region with a rich cultural and historical background and is socially, economically and politically backward, it needs a separate Autonomous Hill Council.[164]

Demand for Autonomous Hill Council by the Muslim-majority districts of Rajouri, Poonch and Doda, as part of a larger plan, to break Jammu's plural identity and reinforce the communal fault line within the Jammu region. The support of the National Conference leaders to these proposals brings back memories of Sheikh Abdullah's plan of

"Greater Kashmir" by isolating two-and-a-half Hindu majority districts of the Jammu region. The claims are in part driven by short term political considerations.[165] The demand for a Pahari region is designed to undermine the influence of the Gujjar and Bakkarwal leaders in the region, because these communities have traditionally backed the Congress Party. Perhaps, that is why Gujjars do not support the demand of an Autonomous Hill Council for Rajouri and Poonch. They believe that, "if the demand is driven by lack of economic development, then the predominantly Hindu hill areas (south of the Chenab in Kathua) have done no better than Rajouri and Poonch. The solution lies in providing a responsive government rather than in sharpening the communal boundaries".[166]

There is another political movement demanding Dogri language inclusion in the eighth schedule of the Indian constitution. The Dogri Sanstha was set up in 1944 which played an important role in preserving folk literature and Dogri miniature paintings, besides holding Dramas and Musharias. The Dogri Sangharsh Morcha supported by several literary social and cultural organisations[167] and Jammu principal political parties has been articulating this demand through processions, demonstration and strikes. Despite the Jammu and Kashmir government's recommendation of the demand for Dogri inclusion in the Eighth Schedule of the Indian constitution, it remains to be conceded by the central government.[168]

Panun Kashmir Movement of Kashmiri Pundits

During 1990's when the militant insurgency started in Kashmir and thousands of people swayed by the conviction that independence was around the corner, were thronging on the streets of Srinagar and chanting the slogan of Azadi. The writ of the state was totally ineffective and the militants were calling shots. The fact that most of the Muslims identified with both the slogan of Azadi as well as with the militants, did not appeal to the sensibilities of the pundits.[169] Also, the Islamisation drive and politicisation of Kashmiri Pundits in early 1990's aroused the political consciousness of this community. Barring a short and abortive attempt of leading the Roti agitation in 1930's, the pundits had traditionally underlined their linguistic and ethnic identity of being Kashmiris. But the exodus from the valley, following the long spell of misery and suffering at migrant camps in Jammu, Delhi and elsewhere, forced the Kashmiri pundits to think of their political interests as separate and different from those of Kashmiri Muslims.[170]

The process of out-migration of the Kashmiri Pundits from the Kashmir Valley started from late 1989, when the militant insurgency started here formally. At that early stage, the urban component was dominated among Kashmiri Pundit Migrants. The migration of Kashmiri Pundits at the initial stage, i.e. from 1989 onwards, was of the community type migration in which all families from particular Mohalla or a Village migrated. The investigation revealed that all Kashmiri Pundits migrated to Jammu and other places in the country with their families, especially women, children and aged. An insignificant number of Kashmiri Pundits left one man, especially of old age and who had good support with local Kashmiris, for taking care of their houses, household things and other belongings.[171] Therefore, so called "migrants" by the administration, the Kashmiri pundits, are in fact refugees in their own country due to total failure of the Indian state to provide security and safety to them, they left their original place. The '*PANUN KASHMIR*' Movement (means our own Kashmir) of Kashmiri Pundits is a struggle to re-conquer Kashmir which is almost lost.[172] '*PANUN KASHMIR*' Movement is an effort to save Kashmiri pundits, to save Kashmir and to save India.[173] Besides being a struggle for survival as a cultural entity and an ancient race, '*PANUN KASHMIR*' is described as a movement for the survival of over 70,000 Kashmiri pundits in their birth land.[174] The Kashmiri Pundits believe that they are original inhabitants of the valley with a distinct sub-culture of the purest class of the Aryans. The Kashmiri Pundits recount centuries of religious, linguistic and political persecution by State rulers. Keeping in mind the centrality of the 'current exodus' in the politicisation of the Pundits, a careful choice of historical episodes is made to single out the instances of Pundits being forced into exile by tyrannical State rulers over the last 650 years.[175]

Punun Kashmir (our own Kashmir) is an organisation of Kashmiri Pundit youth in revolt against the traditionally mellow Pundit leadership as well as the week central leadership in New Delhi. It demanded a separate homeland for Kashmiri pundits consisting of 8,400 sq. km, comprising portions of Anantnag, Baramulla, and Srinagar and Pulwama districts. It constitutes 4 per cent of total area of Jammu and Kashmir State as it existed in August 1947. Jhelum's geographical divide demarcates the "Homeland from the rest of the valley".[176] The homeland is projected as only viable way to secure a cultural outpost for the Pundit community that is in the 'throes of extinction' and protect historical holy shrines and cultural centres of Hindus in Anantnag, Verinag, Bawan, Mattan and Amarnath. Panun Kashmir also seeks union territory status for the Homeland with full application of Indian Constitution in letter and spirit, in order to ensure the right to life, liberty, freedom of expression, faith, equality and rule of law.[177]

However, there does seem to be a genuine desire within Jammu and Kashmir to recover the social capital lost in the last decade and to restore Kashmir's traditional society based on ideas of peaceful coexistence, pluralism and the common syncretic identity of *Kashmiriyat*.[178] New Delhi and the State government in Jammu and Kashmir also seem to have realised that the recovery of this ethos must be central to their efforts to build peace in the state. The return of the Kashmiri Pundit minority community which left Kashmir *en masse* because of the insurgency, is recognised as being vital for the revitalisation of the traditions of pluralism and communal harmony. Indeed, the new government in the state has begun definite plans for a phased return of Pundits to the valley, although this initiative received a setback after a terrorist massacre of twenty four pundits in the Kashmir valley in March 2003.[179]

But from 2005 to 2010, in any case, Pundits were being encouraged to return to Kashmir for festivals, pilgrimages and other special occasions. A dialogue between civil society leaders of Kashmiri Pundits and Kashmiri Muslims is now being promoted and facilitated. Therefore, the return of Pundits is essential for the revitalisation of Kashmiriyat and their return- on terms acceptable to them–continues to be a top priority for the state and Central Governments.[180]

Notes

1. Hintze Hedwig, *Encyclopedia of Social Sciences*, Vol. XII-XIV, New York, Macmillan, 1924, pp. 208-218.
2. Forrester Duncan, B. *Sub- regionalism in India*, Pacific Affairs, Spring 1970, pp. 5-12.
3. *Third Concept,* September 2009, p. 25.
4. Narrain, Iqbal, *Cultural Pluralism, National Integration and Democracy in India*, Asian survey, XVI Oct. 10, 1976, pp. 904-93.

5. Majumdar, A. K. and Bhanwar Singh, (eds.) *Regionalism in Indian Politics*, Radha Publications, New Delhi, 1997, p. 147.
6. *Third Concept*, September 2009, p. 25.
7. Basu Sajal, *Regional Movements: Politics of language, ethnicity and identity*, Indian Institute of Advance Study, Simla, 1992, p. 48.
8. Puri, Balraj, *Sub-Nationalism, Identities and National Integration, Economic and Political Weekly Magazine,* June 1976, pp. 945-48.
9. Mandla Sunita, *Politics of State autonomy and regional identity in J&K,* Delhi, Kalpaz Publisher, 2006, p. 178.
10. Behera, N. C. *State Identity and Violence, Jammu and Kashmir*, Manohar Pub. Delhi, 1999, p. 277.
11. Verma, R. K. *Regionalism and sub-regionalism in state politics social, economic, and political bases,* Deep Publisher, Delhi, 1994, p. 2.
12. *Ibid;* p. 3.
13. *Ibid;* p. 4.
14. Majumdar, A. K. and Bhanwar Singh, (eds.) *Regionalism in Indian Politics*, Radha Publications, New Delhi, 1997, p. 3.
15. Stevenson Garth, *Federalism and Political Economy of Canadian State*, in Leo Panitch (ed.), *The Canadian State: Political Economy and Political Power*, University of Toronto Press, 1977.
16. Majumdar, A. K. and Bhanwar Singh, (eds.) *Regionalism in Indian Politics*, Radha Publications, New Delhi, 1997, p. 3.
17. M. P. Singh and Chandra Mohan (eds.). *Regionalism and Nation Identity Canadian and Indian perspective,* Pragati pub., Delhi, 1994, p. 38.
18. *Ibid;* pp. 38-39.
19. Sunita Mandla, *Politics of State autonomy and regional identity in J&K,* Delhi, Kalpaz Publisher, 2006, p. 178.
20. Majumdar, A. K. and Bhanwar Singh, (eds.) *Regionalism in Indian Politics*, Radha Publications, New Delhi, 1997, p. 47.
21. *Third Concept,* September 2009, p. 25.
22. Majumdar, A. K. and Bhanwar Singh, (eds.) *Regionalism in Indian Politics*, Radha Publications, New Delhi, 1997, p. 156.
23. G.R. Reddy and B. K. Sharma, *Regionalism in India*, Concept publishing company, New Delhi, 1979, p. 3.
24. *Ibid;* p. 4.
25. Narrain, Iqbal, *Regional Politics in India,* P. C. Mathur, *Govt. and Politics in South Asia,* Printwell Pub., Jaipur, 1985, pp. 84-85.
26. Basu, Sajal, *Regional Movements: Politics of language, ethnicity and identity*, Indian Institute of Advance Study, Simla, 1992, p. 48.
27. Chowdhary, Rekha, (ed.) *Identity Politics in Jammu and Kashmir,* Vitasta Publications, New Delhi, 2010, pp. 45-46.

28. Puri, Balraj, *Jammu and Kashmir-Trumph and Tragedy of Indian Federalisation,* Sterling Publishers Pvt. Ltd., 1981, p. 20.
29. Om, Hari, *Special Status in Indian Federation Jammu and Kashmir*, Seema Publication, Delhi, 1983, p. 83.
30. A Pamphlet on *Cultural Heritage of Kashmir,* Srinagar, Kashmir, 1997.
31. Punjabi Riyaz, *Kashmiriyat: The Mystique of an Identity*, IIC Quarterly, New Delhi, Spring, 1991.
32. Puri, Balraj, *Identities, Ideologies and Politics in Jammu and Kashmir State, The Journal of Kashmir Studies Centre,* University of Kashmir Hazratbal Srinagar 2006, Vol.1, pp. 12-14.
33. Sharma, Y. R. *Political Dynamics of Jammu and Kashmir*, Publisher Anand Radhakrishan, Jammu, 2002, pp. 162-163.
34. Wani, Gull, *Kashmir, Kashmiriyat and Sheikh Abdullah*, Daily Kashmir Times, 13 September, 2006.
35. Pampori, M. S. *Kashmir in chains 1819-1992*, Pampori Publishing House, Srinagar, p. 33.
36. Lawrence Walter, *The Valley of Kashmir*, Oxford University Press, 1895, p. 2.
37. Chowdhary Rekha,(ed.), *Identity Politics in Jammu and Kashmir*, Vitasta Publications, New Delhi, 2010, p. 91.
38. Puri, Balraj, *Abdullah Era – Evolution of Kashmiri Identity* (Ed.), 1982, pp. 2-4.
39. Bhushan Vidhaya, *Jammu and Kashmir Politics: Its Critical Aspects*, Yak Publishing Channel, Jammu, 2008, p. 312.
40. Sharma, Y. R. *Political Dynamics of Jammu and Kashmir*, Publisher Anand Radhakrishan, Jammu, 2002, p. 166.
41. Verma, P. S. *Jammu and Kashmir Politics, in the Indian Journal of Political Science, Vol. VVVI, No.* 7, March – Sep. 1987, p. 177.
42. Fazli Manzoor, *Kashmir Predilection (ed.),* Gulshan Publishers, Srinagar, 1988, p. 13.
43. Times of India – Jan 16, 1965.
44. Article 356 deals with the provisions in case of failure of constitutional machinery in states.
45. Article 357 deals with the provision of exercise of Legislative powers under Proclamation issued under article 356.
46. Times of India, January 16, 1965.
47. Fazli Manzoor, *Kashmir Govt. and Politics*, Gulshan Publishers, Srinagar, 1988, p. 13.
48. Puri, Balraj, *Life and work of Sheikh Abdullah*, Kashmir Times, September 20, 1982.
49. Lamb, Alaster, *Kashmir A Disputed Legacy 1846-1990*, Oxford University Press, 1991, p. 313.

50. Sharma, Y. R. *Political Dynamics of Jammu and Kashmir*, Publisher Anand Radhakrishan Jammu, 2002, p. 168.
51. Prakash, Shri and G. M. Shah, *Towards understanding the Kashmir Crisis*, Gyan Publishing House, New Delhi, 2002, p. 158.
52. *Ibid;* pp. 158-159.
53. Ashutosh Varshey, *India, Pakistan and Kashmir- Antinomies of Nationalism*, in *Asian survey Vol. XXXXI No. 11*, Nov. 1991, p. 1015.
54. Sinha Aditya, *Farooq Abdullah Kashmir's Prodigal Son: A Biography*, UBS Publishers, New Delhi, 1995, pp. 180-183.
55. Khan G. H. *Government and politics of Jammu and Kashmir*, light and life publications Jammu p. 431.
56. *Ibid;* pp. 429-430.
57. Schofield, Victoria, *Kashmir in Conflict, India, Pakistan and the unending war*, Viva Books, New Delhi, 2004, pp. 136-137.
58. Verma, P. S. *Jammu and Kashmir at the Political Cross Roads*, New Delhi, 1994, pp. 129-143.
59. Schofield, Victoria, *Kashmir In Conflict, India, Pakistan and the unending war*, Viva Books, New Delhi, 2004, pp. 155-156.
60. Kaur, Ravinderjit, *Why Autonomy to Kashmir*, Institute of Peace and Conflict Studies, September 2003.
61. *Ibid.*
62. Chowdhary, Rekha, (ed.) *Identity Politics in Jammu and Kashmir*, Vitasta Publications, New Delhi, 2010, p. 56.
63. Puri, Balraj, *Identities, Ideologies and Politics in Jammu and Kashmir State, The Journal of Kashmiri Studies*, University of Kashmir, Hazratbal, Srinagar, 2006, pp. 12-13.
64. Prasad, Shri and G. M. Shah (eds.) *Towards Understanding the Kashmir Crisis*, Gyan Publishing House, New Delhi, 2002, pp. 146-147.
65. Puri, Balraj, *Jammu: A Clue to Kashmir Tangle*, 1966, p. 93.
66. Puri, Balraj, *Genesis of Perpetual Regional Tension in Jammu and Kashmir*. Daily Greater Kashmir, Srinagar, Oct. 6, 2009.
67. Chowdhary, Rekha,(ed.) *Identity Politics in Jammu and Kashmir*, Vitasta Publications, New Delhi, 2010, p. 63.
68. Puri, Balraj, *Simmering Volcano study of Jammu's Relations with Kashmir*, Sterling publishers Pvt. Ltd., New Delhi, 1983, p. 9.
69. Kaul, B. L. *Kashmir: Problem and politics*, Seema Publications, 1981, p. 150.
70. Puri, Balraj, *Jammu: A Clue to Kashmir Tangle,* 1966, p. 14.
71. Sharma, Y. R. *Political Dynamics of Jammu and Kashmir*, Publisher Anand Radhakrishan, Jammu, 2002, p. 150.
72. Bazaz, P. N. *Kashmir in Crucible*, Pamposh Publication, New Delhi, 1967, p. 70.

73. Om, Hari, *Special Status in Indian Federation, Jammu and Kashmir*, Seema publication, Delhi, 1983, pp. 112-113.
74. Behera Navnitachadha, *Demystifying Kashmir*, Dering kinderslay (India) Pvt. Ltd., 2007, pp. 108109.
75. Sharma, Y. R. *Political Dynamics of Jammu and Kashmir*, Publisher Anand Radhakrishan, Jammu, 2002, p. 151.
76. *Ibid;* pp. 151-153.
77. Gupta J. B. D. *Jammu and Kashmir*, Martins, Nijihoff, House, 1968, p. 186.
78. Hindustan Times, June 25, 1952.
79. Thomas, R.G.C. (ed.) *Perspectives on Kashmir: The roots of conflict in South Asia*, Boulder colo, West View Press, 1992, p. 213.
80. Akbar, M. J. *Kashmir Behind the Vale*, Roti Books Pvt. Ltd, New Delhi, 2000, p. 143.
81. Sharma, Y. R. *Political Dynamics of Jammu and Kashmir*, Publisher Anand Radhakrishan, Jammu, 2002, p. 151.
82. Bazaz, P. N. *Kashmir in Crucible*, Pamposh Publications, New Delhi, p. 583: Indian Express, December 3, 1952.
83. Om, Hari, *Special Status in Indian Federation, Jammu and Kashmir*, Seema publication, Delhi, 1983, p. 119.
84. Times of India, Feb 3, 1953: Puri, Balraj, *Jammu and Kashmir- An old solution*, The Daily Tribune, June 29, 1977.
85. Sharma, Y. R. *Political Dynamics of Jammu and Kashmir*, Publisher Anand Radhakrishan Jammu, 2002, p. 154.
86 Hindustan Times, August 22, 1953.
87. Sharma, Y. R. *Political Dynamics of Jammu and Kashmir*, Publisher Anand Radhakrishan, Jammu, 2002, p. 154.
88. Behera, Navnita Chadha, *Demystifying Kashmir*, Dering kinderslay (India) Pvt. Ltd. 2007, p. 123.
89. Puri, Balraj, *Simmering Volcano Study of Jammu's Relations with Kashmir*, Sterling publisher Pvt. Ltd, New Delhi, 1983, p. 44.
90. Report, Jammu and Kashmir Commission of Enquiry, Dec 1968, p. 49.
91. Sharma, Y. R. *Political Dynamics of Jammu and Kashmir*, Publisher Anand Radhakrishan, Jammu, 2002, p. 156.
92. Hindustan Times, February 19, 1970.
93. *The Commission of Enquiry* was headed by S. M. Sikri, Retired Chief Justice of the Supreme Court Known as Sikri Commission.
94. *The Sikri Commission report and Regional Imbalances in Jammu and Kashmir,* Srinagar, 1982, pp. 28-31.
95. The Hindu, November 29, 1987.

96. Sharma, Y. R. *Political Dynamics of Jammu and Kashmir*, Publisher Anand Radhakrishan, Jammu, 2002, p. 166.
97. *Report of Regional Autonomy Committee*, Government of Jammu and Kashmir, April 1999, pp. 18-19.
98. Mandla, Sunita, *Politics of state autonomy and regional identity in J&K,* Kalpaz publisher, Delhi, 2006, p. 218.
99. The Tribune, February 13, 2000.
100. Sharma, Y. R. *Political Dynamics of Jammu and Kashmir*, Publisher Anand Radhakrishan, Jammu, 2002, p. 162.
101. Puri, Balraj, *Identities Ideologies and Politics in Jammu and Kashmir state, The Journal of Kashmiri studies,* University of Kashmir, Hazratbal, Sgr. 2006, Vol. I, p. 18.
102. *Ibid;* pp. 18-19.
103. Prakash, S. and G. Mohammad, (eds.) *Towards Understanding The Kashmir Crisis*, Gyan Publishing House, New Delhi, 2002, p. 149.
104. Chowdhary, Rekha, (ed.), *Identity Politics in Jammu and Kashmir*, Vitasta Publications, New Delhi, 2010, pp. 40-41.
105. Kaul, Sridhar and H. Kaul, *Ladakh through the Ages: towards a new identity*, Indus publishing company, New Delhi, 1992, p. 205.
106. Verma, P. S. *Jammu and Kashmir at the Political Cross Roads*, New Delhi, 1994, p. 42.
107. Kaul, Shridhar and H. Kaul, *Ladakh through the Ages: towards a new identity*, Indus publishing company, New Delhi, 1992, p. 209.
108. *Ibid;* p. 210.
109. Sharma, Y. R. *Political Dynamics of Jammu and Kashmir*, Publisher Anand Radhakrishan, Jammu, 2002, pp. 173-174.
110. *Ibid;* p. 174.
111. Indian Express, August 8, 1967.
112. Kak, B. L. *Chasing Shadows in Ladakh*, Light and Life Publishers, New Delhi, 1978, pp. 101-102.
113. *Report of the commission of inquiry*, 1968.
114. Kaul, B. L. *Kashmir: Problems and politics*, Seema Publications, Delhi, 1981, pp. 258-61.
115. *Ibid;* pp. 260-261.
116. Sharma, Y. R. *Political Dynamics of Jammu and Kashmir*, Publisher Anand Radhakrishan, Jammu, 2002, pp. 173-174.
117. Om, Hari and Chowdhary Rekha, (eds.) *Politics of Autonomy in Jammu and Kashmir*, pp. 204-205.
118. The Times of India, December 31, 1980.
119. Matoo, Amitab, Kapil Kak and Happymon Jacob, (eds.) *India and Pakistan: Pathways to Peace*, Pub. K. W. New Delhi, p. 196.

120. *Ibid;* pp. 196-197.
121. Kashmir Times, October 17, 1982.
122. Times of India, May, 1982.
123. Sharma, Y. R. *Political Dynamics of Jammu and Kashmir*, Publisher Anand Radhakrishan, Jammu, 2002, p. 182.
124. *Ibid;* pp. 182-183.
125. Behera, N. Chadha, *Demystifying Kashmir*, Derling Kinderslay, India, 2007, p. 116.
126. *Ibid;* pp. 116-117.
127. Om, Hari, *Ladakhis on the warpath again*, in *Daily Excelsior*, Sep. 10, 1994.
128. Sixth Schedule deals with the provisions as to the administration of Tribal Areas in the states of Assam, Meghalaya, Tripura and Mizoram.
129. Sharma, Y. R. *Political Dynamics of Jammu and Kashmir*, Publisher Anand Radhakrishan, Jammu, 2002, p. 185.
130. Kashmir Times, April 20, 1992.
131. Sharma, Y. R. *Political Dynamics of Jammu and Kashmir*, Publisher Anand Radhakrishan, Jammu, 2002, p. 185.
132. *Ibid;* pp. 185-186.
133. Sharma, Y. R. *Political Dynamics of Jammu and Kashmir*, Publisher Anand Radhakrishan Jammu, 2002, p. 186.
134. The Kashmir Times, August 29, 1994.
135. The Kashmir Times, March 19, 1995.
136. *Ladakh Autonomous Hill Development Council Act,* Government of Jammu and Kashmir, May 1995.
137. The Kashmir Times, February 13, 1997.
138. Sharma, Y. R. *Political Dynamics of Jammu and Kashmir*, Publisher Anand Radhakrishan, Jammu, 2002, p. 188.
139. The Kashmir Times, March 16, 1997.
140. The Kashmir Times, June 6, 2000.
141. Sharma, Y. R. *Political Dynamics of Jammu and Kashmir*, Publisher Anand Radhakrishan, Jammu, 2002, pp. 188-189.
142. *Ibid;* pp. 188-189.
143. Rahi, Javaid, "Gujjars" *Identity Apprehensions and Demands, Daily Rising Kashmir,* Srinagar, October. 2008.
144. Baljit Mann, *Identity Formation, the Jammu and Kashmir Story, Epilogue Magazine* 15 May 2008, Yogesh Pandoh for Epilogue Jammu.
145. Prasad, Shri and G. M. Shah (eds.), *Towards Understanding the Kashmir Crisis*, Gyan Publishing House, New Delhi, 2002, pp. 146-147.
146. *Living in forests and selling milk products*.

147. *Who keeps large herdsd of Bakri-goats.*
148. Lawrence Walter, *The Valley of Kashmir*, Oxford University Press, 1895, pp. 316-317.
149. India's Kashmir war; a report by committee for initiative on Kashmir, New Delhi, March 1990, pp. 43-48.
150. Magray Bashir, *Tribal geography of India – Jammu and Kashmir*, Oberio Book service, Jammu, 2003, p. 90.
151. Khatana, R. P. *Gujri Language and identity in Jammu and Kashmir; Awaz-e-Gujjar,* Jan. 1996, pp.49-54.
152. *Census of India, 1931,* Vol. xxiv, part 11, Jammu and Kashmir.
153. Khatana, R. P. *Gujri Language and identity in Jammu and Kashmir; Awaz-e-Gujjar,* Jan. 1996, pp. 49-54.
154. Behera, N. C. *State, identity and Violence, Jammu Kashmir and Ladakh*, Manohar Publishers, New Delhi, 2000, p. 234.
155. Rafique Anjum, Evolution of Gujri Language: Awa-e-Gujjar, Jan. 1996, pp. 6-12.
156. Khatana, R. R. *Educational Neglect of Gujjar Community: Awaze-e-Gujjar,* June-July 1996, pp. 43-46.
157. Rahi Javaid *Gujjars, Identity Apprehensions and Demands, Daily Rising Kashmir* Srinagar, October. 2008.
158. *Ibid;* Oct. 2008.
159. Puri Balraj, *Identities, Ideologies and Politics in Jammu and Kashmir, Journal of Kashmiri Studies*, University of Kashmir, pp. 17-18.
160. Behera, N. C. *State, identity and Violence, Jammu Kashmir and Ladakh*, Manohar Publishers, New Delhi, 2000, p. 236.
161. Om, Hari and Rekha Chowdhary, *The Politics of Autonomy in Jammu and Kashmir*, pp. 160-161.
162. Maini, K. D. *Facing the challenges Ahead*, Zafar Chowdhary, *Who Patronizes Caste Politics in Rajouri, Poonch,* M. Hussain Malik, *Social Structure and Perceptions of Regional Disparities*, *Epilogue Magazine*, May 2010, issue five, pp. 14-18.
163. Saraf Pushp, *Border Affairs*, Vol. 3, April – June 2008.
164. Behera, N.C. *State, identity and Violence, Jammu Kashmir and Ladakh*, Manohar Publishers, New Delhi, 2000, p. 239.
165. Matoo Amitab, Kapil Kak and Happymon Jacob (eds.), *India and Pakistan: Pathways to Peace*, Pub. K. W., New Delhi. p. 196.
166. Chowdhary Rekha, (ed.) *Identity Politics in Jammu and Kashmir*, Vitasta Publications, New Delhi, 2010, pp. 43-44.
167. These include *Dogri Sanstha, Jammu University Federation, Hindu Rakasha Smiti, Shree Rajput* Youth Federation, and Democratic Youth Federation of India, Jammu Mukti Morcha and Jammu Maha Sabha.

168. Behera, N. C. *State, identity and Violence, Jammu Kashmir and Ladakh*, Manohar Publishers, New Delhi, 2000, pp. 240-241.
169. Lyon Peter, *Conflict between India and Pakistan: An Encyclopedia,* ABC Publications, California, 2008, p. 99.
170. Behera N. C. *State, identity and Violence, Jammu Kashmir and Ladakh*, Manohar Publishers, New Delhi, 2000, p. 226.
171. Dabla Bashir, *Sociological implication of Pandit Migration in Jammu and Kashmir,* pp. 67-68.
172. Samaddur Ranbir, (ed.) *The Politics of Autonomy*, Sage Publications, New Delhi, 2005, p. 153.
173. *Ibid,* pp. 153-154.
174. *Ibid;* pp. 153-154.
175. Destruction of cultural symbols and shrines of Kashmir; issued by Panun Kashmir Movement, website: http//207.159.86.9/atrocities /temples /: Panun Kashmir Demand for Home Land.
176. Pandit, M. L. and T. N. Pandit, *Kashmiri Pandits: A contemporary perspective*, APH publishing corporations, New Delhi, 2005, pp. 35-36.
177. Kaul, Shyan and Onkar Kachru, *Jammu, Kashmir and Ladakh: Ringside Views*, Atlantic publications, New Delhi, 1998, pp. 246-247.
178. Punjabi Riyaz, *Kashmiriyat: The Mystique of an Identity*, IIC Quarterly, New Delhi, Spring 1991.
179. Ganguly Sumit, *The Kashmir Question retrospect and prospect*, Frank CASS, Great Britan, 2003, p. 20.
180. *Ibid;* pp. 20-21.

Chapter - 3

Regional Autonomy Models: A Comparative Study

Regional autonomy according to Yash Ghai, "is a device to allow ethnic or other groups claiming a distinct identity in a particular region to exercise direct control over the affairs of special concern to them, while allowing the larger entity those powers which cover common interests".[1] Timothy D. Sisk identifies ten distinct "conflict regulating practices/models", half of them falling under the heading of "Consociational" approach, the other half under the heading of "integrative" approach. A Consociational power sharing approach freely recognises and represents separate ethnic groups, while an integration approach adopts practices that downplay separate ethnic group identity in favour of cross-cutting individual interests usually economic.[2] The practice of autonomy on the Consociational side, classify it among the "territorial divisions of power". It is the basis to accommodate the ethnic minority groups through the grants of regional autonomy or ethnic autonomy to the minority group.[3] Generally speaking, there are two different kinds of autonomy, territorial and non-territorial or cultural. Non-territorial autonomy clearly has relevance in circumstances where the ethnic group is fairly small, weak or territorially dispersed. As far as territorial autonomy is concerned, it is an arrangement aimed at granting to a group, a means by which it can express its distinct identity, that differs from the majority of the population in the state, but that constitutes the majority in a specific region.[4] However, there are other arrangements also in addition to territorial autonomy to secure the diffusion of power. Lapidoth identifies five of them as federal systems, decentralisation, self-government, associate statehood and self–administration. Ruth Lapidoth writes that the Frame Work for Peace in Middle-East, the 1978 Camp David Accord between Egypt and Israel referred to 'full autonomy' for the Palestinian Arabs, whereas in subsequent negotiations the preferred term has been 'self rule' or 'self government'.[5] The differences among these terms are not in all cases trivial, however, all of them do not attach the same importance to the maintenance and promotion of a distinct identity. While Autonomy seems to imply less self-rule than does the term confederalism, for instance, it is generally understood to imply greater-self - rule than federalism which, as in the American case, need not cater to ethnic group identities at all. In the face of the common Indian assertion that Kashmir's separatist inclinations can be adequately satisfied within the context of a reinvigorated Indian federalism.

However, since 2000, the idea of ethnic or regional autonomy had clearly gained considerable ground internationally, as a legitimate device for conflict resolution.[6] An analyst of ethnic conflict Ted Robert Gurr, offered the starting observation, "that a global consensus in regard to the handling of inter-group relations in ethnically mixed societies already existed by then, and that this consensus was paying off with a measurable diminution in ethnic warfare."[7] He also claimed that, a major strategic shift from confrontation to accommodation was under way. The government repertories of ethnic conflict management, hitherto heavily emphasising repression had consciously been expanded to include minority group rights and various forms of autonomy. However, lending additional weight to regional autonomy's acceptability, were a number of concrete examples of its apparently successful incorporation in state practice, as in the 1979 Home Rule Act of the Danish parliament granting substantial Self rule to Greenland or, as in 1999, the concession by the United Kingdom of a separate Scottish Parliament. The conference on the Human Dimension, in Copenhagen in June 1990, also identified regional autonomy model as a mechanism for ensuring balanced socio-economic development and the protection of human rights.[8]

The territorial regional autonomy hitherto has been established in at least 21 countries. As some states are home to more than one autonomous region for instance, Spain has seventeen autonomous communities; Italy has five regions with special autonomy, Great Britain three, Nicaragua and Portugal two etc. There are at least 60 regions in the world vested with territorial autonomy with scientifically based criteria.[9] Regional autonomy is successfully operating in Aland Island since 1921, got the special status within Finland, while, the most recent autonomy, is that of the province of Aceh in Indonesia which was approved by the Indonesian Parliament in June 2006. The basic feature of these working autonomies has been illustrated in "The World's Working Regional Autonomies". In fact, in the scientific literature there is still no comparative empirical evaluation of the results produced by these specific arrangements, following the model of comparative studies. Yet, comparisons often are barred by the assumed "uniqueness" of every autonomy system and same is said for attempts to suggest solutions transferring certain models of autonomy arrangements to other similar conflict areas.[10] Therefore, according to Prof. Rehmatullah, "it is true that all the working autonomies have been created against a specific social, political, cultural, ethnic background, based on unique historical and political genesis and aimed to accommodate the needs and interests of specific groups living in these areas and minority people within a state. There are many examples which shows that regional autonomy can be established in federalised lines without disturbing the national unity to accommodate the interests of minorities or regions who are demanding for autonomies with special needs e.g. Belgium, Ethiopia, Philippines, Indonesia, Georgia, Spain, Nigeria, Canada, etc".[11]

The Indian experience with reference to regional autonomy is the most instructive because of its diversity and range, the extent of colonial innovations, multiple forms of autonomy, the complex path of constitutionalism, a wide variety of accords, the persistent demands for self-determination in various forms and an unyielding and innovative state determined to keep the destined nation intact. While keeping others from gaining statehood, the constitution provides special status for certain states such as Jammu and Kashmir, Nagaland, Sikkim, Assam, Manipur and Arunachal Pradesh under Articles 370 to 371.[12] There are also provisions regarding the establishment of Zonal Councils, Autonomous District Councils in Schedule Tribe dominated districts. The 73rd and 74th amendments to the constitution ensured devolution of powers at village and town levels. Similarly, the constitution arranged for financial autonomy of the states through constitutionally prescribed division of resources.[13] Also, there are some Hill Councils operating to check the regional imbalances and socio-economic needs from far flung and hilly areas e.g. Darjeeling, Bodoland, Leh, North Cachar Hills, Karbi Anglong District, Tripura Tribal Areas district, Chakma, Mara and La District Councils under Fifth and Sixth Schedule.[14]

Broadly speaking, Jammu and Kashmir state consists of three distinctively geographical regions—Kashmir, Jammu and Ladakh. The three regions are not only three dissimilar geographical entities but in regard to history and culture they are also different from one another.[15] Indeed, Jammu and Kashmir is a deeply divided state fragmented along regional, religious and ethnic differences. Inter-regional and inter-religious tensions became pronounced immediately after Jammu, Kashmir and Ladakh were welded into a single political entity with full backing of the colonial power. As the Jammu Dogra rulers were fundamentally despotic, feudal and sectarian, the Muslims of the State got alienated and fought a struggle against the Dogra domination which culminated in the termination of Dogra Raj in 1947. However, till date the Dogras did not compromise with this, what they regarded humiliation to their collective pride.[16] It is not therefore, surprising that they harbor the dreams of carving out a separate state for Jammu and the anti-Kashmiri sentiment has become a fertile ground for 'conflict entrepreneurs' of Hindutva forces. But this sentiment is restricted among the Hindu populated areas of the Jammu province as the Muslims refuse to be a part of this discourse. In fact, they demand sub-regional autonomy to safeguard their political, cultural and economic interests from the monopolistic political tradition-the aspiration reflected in the Autonomy Report of National Conference.[17] This voice has become louder since the eruption of Jammu agitation sponsored by Hindutva forces in August 2008. The counter demands to the establishment of Central University at Samba, the centre of communal forces by Muslim leaders of Muslim dominated subregions of Jammu and regional polarisation over the issue of Land row controversy over Amarnath further testify to the beginning of their mounting identity activism. Therefore, in order to meet the inter-regional problems in Jammu and Kashmir, the number of commissions and committees have been appointed from time to time and number of models/proposal have been drafted to meet the inter-regional problems.[18]

Regional Autonomy Model of National Conference

The regional autonomy has been one of the perennial debates in Jammu and Kashmir State in the post independent India. The principle of regional autonomy was accepted by the popular leadership of the state both before the independence in its famous constitutional document 'Naya Kashmir' as well as immediately after the state acceded to the Union of India in 1947.[19] In his address to the Constituent Assembly on 11th August, 1952, providing the details about the Delhi Agreement, Sheikh Mohammad Abdullah said that he was committed to give, "maximum autonomy for the local organs of the state power which are the ultimate source of authority in the state while discharging obligations as a unit of the federation".[20] In a broadcast from Radio Kashmir, Srinagar on 17th April, 1953, Sheikh Mohammad Abdullah made it clear that the State Government will abide by its decision to "give autonomy to the different cultural units (emphasis added) of the state as would be provided in the constitution that is drawn up".[21] He further said that, "this would remove all the fears of discrimination of one unit over the other and will make for the voluntary unity and consolidating of the people of the State".[22]

As the internal autonomy and balanced development has been a constant demand of different ethno-cultural linguistic groups, the state government had earlier appointed two important commissions, Gajendragadkar Commission and Sikri Commission, to suggest measures to redress the grievances and meet the identity aspirations of different regions and sub-regions of the state.[23] Moreover, the militancy in Jammu and Kashmir rose after the rigged elections of 1987. When the number of Kashmiri youth crossed over the line of control for getting arms training in Pakistan and induction of arms and ammunition in the valley started. After the eruption of militancy in 1989, the Indian government promised autonomy once again. The objective behind this offer was to check the secessionist trend in Kashmir and create a favourable situation for the pro-accession parties and hold the elections. Though the situation was not favourable, yet dates for the parliamentary elections were fixed in 1996.[24] The major regional and pro-accession party of the state, the Jammu and Kashmir National Conference, threatened to boycott these elections as its President Farooq Abdullah insisted that the quantum of autonomy should be decided before the polls. However, the Central Government remained adamant that the question of autonomy would be decided with the elected representatives of the state and within this package of autonomy, the quantum of regional autonomy for the three regions of the state was also taken into consideration.[25]

Farooq Abdullah after winning the Assembly elections, in 1996 concentrated on his first priority of defining, deciding and negotiating a package of autonomy for the three regions of the state.[26] For this purposes, the Jammu and Kashmir government has constituted a committee, headed by Chief Minister, Dr. Farooq Abdulla as Chairman and Shri Balraj Puri as its Working Chairman on November 29,1996, to recommend ways and means for regional autonomy to the three regions/provinces of this state. The Regional Autonomy Committee Report prepared under Balraj Puri became controversial when it was found that without discussing the report with the committee members, Mr. Puri went public on it and leaked it out to the press. Another limitation of the report was its sweeping recommendations of having a five tier system of governance ranging from State to Panchayats. Its implementation would have in the ultimate analysis left the state government with no powers. Further, as some members claimed that certain memoranda that had come from district Doda of Jammu and Kashmir were not taken into account by Shri Balraj Puri. In view of the seriousness of these issues Balraj Puri was removed from the working Chairmanship of Regional Autonomy Committee. The Committee under the Chairmanship of Farooq Abdullah prepared a new report which eventually became the official report of the government.[27] The terms of reference of the committee were:

1. To examine, consistent with the integrity of the state and to promote better involvement and participation of people in different regions for balanced political, economic, educational, social and cultural development, evolving of instrumentalities, like local organs of power, at all levels.
2. To examine the powers that such organs need to be vested with to achieve the objective set above.
3. To examine whether any change in the state constitutional structure, obtaining as at present, is required.

However, Regional Autonomy Committee explained that there is a "sharp sense of neglect and discrimination among the diverse ethnic hilly and far–flung areas of the Jammu province" and that "there is a strong case for the decentralisation of political and economic power which can be achieved through autonomy of the regions of the state", the committee made the recommendation for the reconstruction of two provinces of Jammu and Kashmir.[28] The Committee felt that there is a dire urgency of defining the regions/provinces in the state to achieve the twin objectives of self governance and rapid social development because the prevailing classification of provinces/divisions was hampering the process of social/human development as well as democratic participation at the grassroots level within the state. Thus, in view of historical, social, ethnic and development factors, the Committee recommended that the existing two provinces/divisions of Jammu and Kashmir should be classified into the following eight new regions.[29]

Regional/Provincial Councils (Model – I)

The Regional Autonomy Committee recommended the establishment of Regional/Provincial Councils in the state to meet the requirements of devolution of power to different Regions/Provinces in the state. The constitution and the functions of these councils as suggested by the committee were:[30]

1. The Regional/Provincial councils should be elected in the same manner in which the state legislature is elected. The delimitation of the constituencies should be carried out by the State Election Commission constituted for this purpose. The number of constituencies should be determined in a manner that at least two members from each Block are elected to the Council according to the Constituencies delimited for this purpose.
2. There should be a reservation of 25 per cent seats for women in the Council.
3. The leader of the majority party so elected in the Region/ Province shall head the Regional/Provincial Councils and be designated as Chief Executive Councilor. He/She shall have a status of Minister of the state; He/She shall not have more than four Executive Councillors to aid and assist him.
4. The establishment of Regional/Provincial councils shall, in no way, effect the institutions of the state, viz; Governor,

Chief Minister and his Cabinet, Legislative Assembly, Judiciary and state cadre of services. These institutions shall continue as they are.

5. The Regional/Provincial Councils shall enjoy the executive and taxation powers which should be limited to the subjects allocated to the Council. These subjects should be allocated keeping in view the specificities of Jammu and Kashmir State. In this behalf the experience of District Councils established elsewhere in the country could provide some guidance. However, this matter needs to be examined carefully by the Committee of experts which may be constituted separately. There is equally a need to amend the state constitution which would define the powers of the council as well as provide the mechanism of transferring of items from one list to another i.e. from the state to Regional/Provincial list or vice versa. There is also a need to evolve a mechanism to deal with the situation where the Regional/Provincial Council has lost the Majority, or has failed to carry on its functions within the provisions of the state constitution, or is working against the interests of the state or country.
6. It is well recognised that political autonomy is tethered to financial autonomy. As this would be first ever experiment of this nature in the country, the selection of subjects to be dealt with by the Regional/Provincial Councils and the areas of allocation of funds and powers of taxation etc. need to be worked out carefully. It is equally a fact that different Regions/ Provinces of the state do not face uniform problems. For instance, the development problems of Nund Abad region[31] and the problems of Maraz[32] are not the same. In the same vein, the development problems which these Regions/ Provinces face are not similar to the problems of Chenab valley region. The basic objective of regional autonomy is to replace the mechanisms and processes of centralised decision making in governance and decentralised process and mechanisms. However, the quest to evolve new mechanisms should not lead to the creation of new centralised institutions which would hamper the social development in the Regions and Provinces. The committee is of the view that patterns of

financial autonomy of Panchayati Raj Institutions as prevailing in other states of India be further studied and a model for the financial autonomy of the Regional/Provincial Councils may be evolved. An expert committee may be constituted to propose a model for financial autonomy for the councils.

District Councils (Model – II)

The committee suggested in its approach paper that more than one approach may be adopted in dealing with the issue of internal autonomy in the state. The committee, therefore, recommended that the government may consider setting up District Councils as an alternative to the Regional/Provincial Councils. In view of the experience of District Councils elsewhere in the country, the committee feels that the Councils in co-ordination with Panchayat Raj Institutions can be effective agents in augmenting the processes leading to foster pace of human development, besides providing effective organs of local self-government. The state has been a forerunner in introducing the concept of 'District Planning' by initiating 'single line administration' in the year 1976.[33] The system was introduced to meet the aspirations of the common man by making the planning more effective and ensuring the speedy implementation of development programmes. In order to further democratise the system, the District Development Commissioners were replaced by Ministers of the Cabinet as chairpersons of District Development Boards. The committee is of the view that this experiment has been quite fruitful. The establishment of District Councils shall, drawing upon this experience, completely democratize the processes of planning and development at the district level. The committee, therefore, recommended that in case this model of internal autonomy is accepted, suitable amendment in the constitution of the state should be carried out.[34]

The committee suggested some measures for the constitution of the District Councils. The District Councils should be elected in the same manner in which the State legislature is elected. The delimitation of the constituencies should be carried out by the State Election Commission constituted for this purpose. The number of constituencies should be determined in a manner that at least two members from each block are elected from the constituencies delimited for this purpose.[35] There should be a reservation of 25 per cent seats for women in the council. The leader of the majority party in the Council shall be designated as Chief Councillor and shall have the status of Minister of the State. He/She shall have not more than four Executive Councillors to aid and assist him/her.[36]

The District Councils shall enjoy the executive and taxation powers which should be limited to the subjects allocated to the Council. These subjects should be allocated keeping in view the specificities of Jammu and Kashmir State. In this regard, the experience of District Councils functioning elsewhere in the country could provide some guidance. The committee also recommends that an Experts Committee, proposing the subjects to be allocated to the District Councils, be constituted.[37]

The committee also recommends the evolving of mechanisms to deal with the transfer of subjects from the state list to district list and vice versa. There is also need to evolve the mechanism of dealing with a situation where the leader of the majority party has lost the majority in the Council, or has failed to carry on its functions within the provisions of the state constitution, or working against the interests of the state or country.

The committee recommends that the issue relating to the allocation of funds and the powers of taxation may be assigned to a committee of experts which should be constituted for this purpose. It needs to be recognised that the problems of development of different districts are not uniform.[38]

Culture and Autonomy

The Committee recognises the aspirations of ethnic identities in seeking the avenues of flourishing their culture and languages. The cultural identities have a great potential in consolidating social cohesion and transcending the religious boundaries in plural societies. The multiple cultural identities located in different regions in the state should be provided the opportunities to thrive.[39]

The academy of Art, Culture and Languages has been established in the state in terms of Article 146 (Part–XI) of the constitution of Jammu and Kashmir. According to this provision, the state has to provide opportunities for the development of Art and Culture of the state and for the development of Hindi, Urdu and other regional languages of the state specified in the Sixth Schedule. The Sixth Schedule specifies Kashmiri, Dogri, Balti (Pali), Dardi, Punjabi, Pahari and Ladakhi as regional languages.[40]

This committee recommends that the Jammu and Kashmir Academy of Art, Culture and Languages should establish its proposed Regional/Provincial or District Cultural Offices at Regional/Provincial or District levels. The academy should specific funds to these cultural offices. These offices shall function under the supervision and administrative control of Regional/Provincial or District Councils. There is a dire need of drawing the mosaic of diverse cultures, languages, and dialects of the state. The cultural offices at the Regional/Provincial or District levels would be advised to draw these profiles to project the diversity of the state.[41]

The committee also recommends the constituting of an inter-Regional/Provincial or District Councils to recommend the measures to Jammu and Kashmir Academy of Art, Cultural and Languages to promote different cultural traditions, languages and dialects. The Committee further recommends that the recommendations of inter–Regional/Provincial or District Councils should be binding on the Academy.

The electronic media is playing a major role in promoting the languages and cultures world over. The linguistic identities in the state are keen that they are represented in these media. The delegation of different linguistic groups and the memorandums submitted by them to the committee bring forth the urge of linguistic identities to be represented in the electronic media. The committee is well aware that the institutions of Radio and Doordarshan are not within the administrative control of the state government. However, the committee recommends that the government should approach the concerned authorities in the central government in ensuring that these languages are duly and effectively represented in the media.[42]

The committee also recommends that the Academy of Art, Culture and Languages should provide financial assistance to the cultural and linguistic organisations of different languages in the state in order to provide them opportunities to thrive and develop these cultures and languages.

The Gojari language has been recognised by the state Academy of Art, Culture and Languages as the second language. The committee recommends that this language be included in the Sixth Schedule of the constitution of the state.[43]

The Committee feels that Urdu, being official language of the state, deserves a special attention. The committee recommends that a committee of well known Urdu writers, authors and poets be formed to give a report on the present status of Urdu language in the state. The committee further recommends that the Academy of Art, Culture and Languages should evolve effective mechanisms in coordinating with the nodal agency which has been set up by the Union Minister of Human Resources Development for the promotion of Urdu.

The State Government has introduced a scheme of language orientation for the teachers in the state. Under this scheme, it is compulsory for Urdu knowing teachers to learn Hindi and vice versa. The Committee recommends that the state Departments of School Education should monitor the effective implementation of the scheme. The committee further recommends that this scheme should be extended to the officials of the government. To begin with, a particular level of the officials may be identified which could be later extended to the other vertically and horizontally.[44]

The Autonomy Report was tabled in the Assembly in April 1999 by then Chief Minister Farooq Abdullah and it was decided that an Action Taken Committee would be constituted with Prof. Reyaz Punjabi as the convener. Many Seminars, both official and unofficial, were held at Jammu and Srinagar in order to elicit the opinion of experts and the political parties on the issue of regions and regional autonomy but till date no Action Taken Report has be prepared.[45]

Balraj Puri's Regional Autonomy Model

Balraj Puri was born in 1928. He is the leading Indian political commentator and human rights activist from Jammu. Balraj Puri is one name quite well in the intellectual circles of India for his thought-provoking ideas and vast knowledge of political and social problems of the country. Mr. Puri has made a monumental contribution to the history of the State of Jammu and Kashmir. He is the main spokesman of autonomies for Jammu and Ladakh. He believes that the only regional autonomy within Jammu and Kashmir state would end the on-going agony of the state and bring close the three regions which have distinct cultures and historical backgrounds. His keen interest on the regional autonomy to Jammu and Kashmir has led him to draft his "own model of Regional Autonomy" which latter on was published in the form of book, "Jammu and Kashmir Regional Autonomy Report, 1999".[46]

Balraj Puri met Pundit Jawaharlal Nehru on April 14, 1952, and he presented a memorandum to Prime Minister, while supporting the claim of the Kashmiri leaders for a special status within the Union of India and Ladakh on the other hand demanding union territory status, Jammu wanted complete merger with union, Mr. Puri demanded autonomous status for the three constituent units of Kashmir, Ladakh and Jammu in the state constitution.[47] The Autonomy Forum under the leadership of Mr. Balraj Puri has, however, remained consistent with its demand of regional autonomy. He had several meetings with Pundit Jawaharlal Nehru and other leaders to press his view point.[48] He submitted detailed memoranda to the Gajendragadkar Commission and Sikri Commission. The number of articles he has written and got published in both the local and the National Press all these years bear a testimony to his untiring efforts to arrive at an acceptable and honourable solution of the Kashmir problem.

With the return of Sheikh Abdullah to power in 1975 after remaining in jail for about 23 years. It was hoped that he would attempt to put the regional autonomy demand into action. In those days the National Conference published a pamphlet entitled "WHY NATIONAL CONFERENCE", it contained a categorical statement that the party proposes to reorganise the internal set up of the state on the basis of federal structure which would provide Regional autonomy and further decentralisation of political power through appropriate constitutional arrangements at district, blocks and village levels. The regional autonomy was also a written part of Indira Gandhi- Sheikh Abdullah Accord which brought the later to power in the state. On the eve of his swearing-in-ceremony as Chief Minister Sheikh Abdullah told Jammu and Kashmir Pradesh Congress Legislative Party, on the support on which he resumed his office, on 24th July, 1975. He said, "on my part, I will make a sincere effort to ensure that all the three regions not only have equal opportunity for full and speedy development but that the people in every part of the state have a full participation in the political affairs of the state".[49] Though, Sheikh Abdullah reiterated his commitment to grant regional autonomy at number of times after returning to power in 1974. His son and successor Dr. Farooq Abdullah also did the same, but for some reason or the other, it remained unimplemented till Farooq Abdullah formed his government after winning an election inter alia on the issue of regional autonomy, in 1996.

Again in November 1996, Farooq Abdullah and his government set up the regional autonomy committee to re-examine the issue of inter-regional relations with Balraj Puri as its working chairman. Balraj Puri as the working chairman of the Regional Autonomy Committee appointed by the Jammu and Kashmir government sent a draft report to all its members, including the Chief Minister on June 9, 1998 for favour of their kind considerations, scrutiny and comments. Despite a reminder, he did not receive any comment. It could be a fair conclusion that none had any serious disagreement with any part of the report. He requested the Chief Minister to call a meeting for finalising the report.[50] Balraj Puri received a letter from the Chief Secretary on 21 January, 1999 that his term expired on 31 December, 1998. Through another order Dated 4 March 1999, the term of the committee minus Balraj Puri extended and an alternate twenty eight page report was hastily got drafted. Later on, Balraj Puri published the Regional Autonomy committee report in the form of a book and coming up with his own model of regional autonomy. It consists of broad outlines of political autonomy, cultural autonomy and financial autonomy.[51]

Political Autonomy

However, despite many inadequacies in the report of the Gajendragadkar Commission, it recognised the paramountancy of political aspirations and pertinently observed; "even if all matters were equitably settled, we feel that there would be a measure of discontent unless the political aspirations of the different regions of the state are satisfied. In fact, we consider that the main cause of irritation and tension is the feeling of political neglect and discrimination, real or imagined, from which certain regions of the state suffer".[52] In fact, the basic feature of regional autonomy or a federal setup is sharing of power and functions between the central authority and its constituent parts. In Jammu and Kashmir, the regional autonomy committee envisages a federal structure not only for the state but for the regions also i.e., further devolution of power, from centre to state, state to regions, regions to districts, and districts to local bodies.[53]

The regional autonomy committee under Balraj Puri suggested that the state level institutions, viz. governor, chief minister and his cabinet, legislative assembly, judiciary and state cadre services shall continue as they are. They shall continue to deal with all subjects except those delegated to the regions. The basic criteria for division of subjects is that all subjects that need a uniform policy for the whole state can be handled more efficiently at the state level, involve expenditure beyond the financial capacity of the regions, its benefits transcend regional boundaries and deal with inter-regional problems shall be allotted to the state. Likewise, in preparing the list of regional subjects, the twenty nine subjects allocated to districts in other parts of the country, according to 73rd amendment of the constitution, plus subjects of inter-district importance and are within the financial reach of the regions should be included. The committee also recommended that Article 249 of the Indian constitution may be added in the constitution of the state which may permit, with the consent of regional legislatures, transfer of subjects from one list to another. The committee proposed that at this stage, only a regional list of subjects be drawn and residuary powers should remain with the state. Also, the state constitution may include a provision similar to Article 356 of the Indian constitution empowering the state government to recommend to the governor to take the functions of a regional government if it can't be carried on in accordance with the provisions of the state constitution. Moreover, there should be a statutory provision for fresh election within six months in case a regional council is dissolved.[54]

The model also recommends a change in the legislative council of the state. According to Balraj Puri, "Jammu and Kashmir have equal representation in the legislative council except that out of Kashmir's share two seats are reserved for Ladakh. This is unfair to Kashmir region. It is, therefore, suggested that regional legislatures of Jammu and Kashmir elect equal number of members namely, eleven each to the state legislative council. Ladakh would be too big a jump from its present quota of two and others will be the same as it is. The objective of equity may be served if it is triplicated with fair representation to its geographical and communal diversity. Also, each region should have its own divisional commissioner and IGP to administer the region".[55]

However, with reference to regional level institutions, the regional autonomy committee suggested that regional government should be elected in the same manner in which the state or national government is elected. A Regional legislature which may be called regional council should be elected from twice the number of constituencies as are for the State Assembly, delimited by the same Election Commission which does it for the State. To differentiate the state and regional set up, the members of the regional cabinet may be called executive council and their head be named chief executive council and having a status of a Cabinet Minister of the State.

The legislative, executive and taxation powers of the regional councils shall be limited to the subjects allocated to the regions. And without executive powers, an autonomous authority has no meaning. As for as taxation is concerned, Panchayat be granted these powers through the 73rd and 74th amendment to the Indian constitution.[56] Just as regional autonomy is essential to strengthen the unity of the state, same degree of autonomy to the districts is also necessary to maintain unity and harmony of the regions. It is for this reason that the entire debate of regional autonomy in the state has been linked with a five tier system and includes devolution of power from region to district, blocks and Panchayat.[57] Jammu and Kashmir Panchayat Raj Act of 1989 defines the powers and functions of the three tier institutions of the Panchayat Raj. The amendments to it, to meet the elementary requirements of democracy and those of multi-ethnic and multi–religious character of Jammu and Kashmir state as also to make it an organic part of the system of regional autonomy is necessary.[58]

While the Panchayat Raj Acts of all the states of India and 73rd amendment of the Indian constitution provide for direct elections of most of the Panchayat Raj institutions in the Jammu and Kashmir law, not a single member of district board is directly elected. Even the chairman of the board is nominated by the government. This is clearly the negation of democratic principles and deprives the districts of the status and power that are necessary to make them an effective link in the chain of regional autonomy institutions.[59] The model also recommends that the district councils should have the same supervisory and coordinating the power over block committees and Panchayats as regional council have over districts or the state government has over regional councils. Also, each district council should have a right to send one representative to the regional council. Moreover, it also recommends further extending the process of internal autonomy to

Block Committee and Halqa Panchayats.[60] So far as the urban areas are concerned, the municipalities and corporations should also be brought within the framework of the proposed decentralised set up. The municipalities should function under the supervision and control of regional councils.[61]

Cultural Autonomy

A rational and well thought cultural policy is of special importance for a multi-ethnic state. Culture is the most creative and effective means of assertion of an ethnic identity. Cultural autonomy of each ethnic identity within a framework of multiculturalism, as it is called, is a far better guarantee of unity as well as of enrichment of human life. So, cultural avenues of self expression and legitimate pride are necessary pre-requisites of a viable political system. That is why the institutions of cultural autonomy and development, therefore, assume special significance.[62]

The model drafted by Balraj Puri suggests an independent ministry of culture to deal with diversity and complicity of the cultural problems of the state of Jammu and Kashmir be set up. Similarly, cultural academy is trifurcated on the national pattern to deal with language and literature, theatre and music and fine arts respectively like Sahitya Academy, Sangeet Natak Academy and Lalit Kala Academy. Each need a specialised treatment and no single person and an institution can be expected to have expertise and command over all branches of culture; particularly at this stage when work of each branch has expanded in our state. The Cultural academies need a full attention and autonomy. These should be headed by a non-government. Whole time and competent personality in his/her field. The model also focuses on the other dimensions i.e., the academy should at least work according to its existing statute. For instance, the general council and central committee should meet regularly as directions provided. Moreover, the entire cultural offices need not to move along with the annual durbar move. Some of its work should be transferred to its regional office.[63]

The committee suggested that there is need to set up a full-fledged Department of Translation either in the universities or separately. Its task should be to translate selected literatures of various languages of the state into one another as also to translate some of the world classics into or the other language used in the state. In case of central media and Television, the state should recommend to the centre for the formation of Programme advisory committees for different languages. The committee also suggested that, "the information and Broadcasting Ministry should also be requested that the name of Radio Kashmir Jammu should be changed to Jammu and Kashmir Radio Jammu. For full name of the state should be used and not of a region; as by new regional consciousness has grown so much that omission of Jammu in the name of the Radio Station hurts the sentiments of the people of Jammu. And by now, Kashmir's status as a distinct region has also been well established within the state."

The present proposed model also recommends a four language formula unlike the rest of the country which has adopted three language formulas. The four languages include Mother tongue, Urdu, Hindi and English to be taught at different levels. The committee also recommended that the languages Hindi, Kashmiri, Dogri, Gojjari, Pahari, Punjabi, Bodhi, Sheena and Baderwahi should also be promoted.[64]

Financial Autonomy

Political autonomy can hardly work if financial allocations are arbitrary and if power of fund raising and suspending and policy decisions regarding priorities remain centralised. It is also true in vice versa. For, financial autonomy can neither be achieved nor maintained without political empowerment of decentralisation of institutions. In fact, developmental imbalances are the main issue of political protest in the state.[65]

According to Balraj Puri, economic backwardness is arguably an important cause of popular unrest. But more than absolute backwardness, it is relative deprivation that causes heart burning; particularly if it is due to real or perceived policies of discrimination. The developmental outlays in different regions and within regions should, therefore, be basically governed by two criteria viz. equity and objectivity and not governed by political, subjective and arbitrary considerations. Traditional approach of measuring respective prosperity and poverty of different regions, based on regional or per capita income and rate of growth have been found inadequate and inaccurate. Moreover, equal regional or per capita government investments would not be equitable. If equal allocations are made for finance on construction of a road, for instance, in plains of Jammu or of Kashmir valley as are made for a hilly area of, say Doda or far off place like Zanaskar, it will not yield the same results and will, therefore, not be fair. Therefore, this model suggests an alternative approach to achieve the objective of equity. That is special note taken by the United Nations Human Development Programme. According to the report of Human development 2005 regarding, "many faces of poverty", "It is much more than low income. It also reflects poor health and communication, inability to exercise human and political rights and the absence of dignity, confidence and self respect. There is also environmental impoverishment. Behind these faces of poverty lies the grim reality of desperate lives without choice and often governments that lack capacity to cope".[66]

Apart from equity, the second criteria of a financial policy of the state are objectivity. For this purpose, the committee laid down an objectively determinable and verifiable formula, for sharing the finances of the state. However, its application should not be left to the discretion of political autonomous regions and of other extra-regional levels. Also, under Article 370 of the Indian constitution, the state Assembly should incorporate it in the constitution of the state with further amendment that the State Finance Commission will determine the sharing of resources between the state and of regions on the basis of a prescribed formula. The same formula should apply to intra-regional devolutions of funds.[67]

Outlines for criteria of sharing of funds between state and regions;

1. Total state receipts

A. Receipts of the state; internal revenue.

I Revenue Account:

(a) Taxes

(b) Non Tax Revenue: Power Development Board, Road Transport Corporations, Public Sector Undertakings, Mining and Forests.

II Capital account:

(a) Unfunded debt

(b) Recovery of loans.

B. Transfer from the centre

1. Statutory grants
2. Share in central taxes
3. Non-plan grants
4. Central schemes
5. Centrally sponsored schemes transferred to the state with funds.
6. Earmarked schemes
7. Loans from the centre.

C. Negotiated loans and market borrowings.

2. Receipts of the regions

A. Grants:

Total receipts of the state are shared with the regions in 50:50 ratios. Out of the share of the state five per cent be allocated to the regions on the discretion of the State Government to meet contingencies, natural calamities and special needs of some areas in addition to the regional share of revenue.

State Share of Grants

While citing the example of Kerala state government has allocated 40 per cent of the state's total resources to the Panchayat Raj institutions. As regional tier is proposed to be added the allocation to regions, including Panchayat Raj institutions has been raised to 55 per cent out of which 5 per cent would be at the discretion of the state govt. The share of each region to be determined on a formula based on the following indicators:-

1. Population.
2. Area.
3. Road Mileage; surface road divided by area.
4. Share in Government jobs as percentage of population in the relevant age group.
5. Average annual admission in last five years to technical institutions as percentage of population in the relevant age group.
6. Female literacy.
7. Infant mortality.

Formula for Allocation of Grants

Allocation to a region should be sum total of ranking of these seven indices divided by the sum total of indices for the three regions, multiplied by resources available for distribution. Similarly, share of district X1 within a region will be equal to

$$\frac{Ix}{I_1+I_2+I_3+I_4+\ldots\ldots In} X R$$

$$Ix \text{ (Index for District x)} = x_1 + x_2 + x_3 + x_4 + \ldots\ldots x_8$$

X_1 to X_8 are ranks for a district in terms of variables 1 to 8 and R denotes total resources available to the state for distribution as grants while n represents number of districts. $I_1 + I_2 + I_3 + I_4 + \ldots\ldots$ In are indices for the districts within a region.

Variables

1. Female literacy — Rank in ascending order. I for least illiteracy and n for highest illiteracy
2. Infant Mortality — Rank in ascending order. I for lowest and n for highest
3. Road mileage divided by area — Rank in descending order. I for highest mileage and n for lowest mileage
4. Share in government services divided by population in the age group 18 to 50 — Rank in descending order. I for highest and n for lowest
5. Share in admission to technical institutions
   a. Medical
   b. Engineering
   c. M.B.A. — … Do…
   d. Agriculture divided by population in the age Group of 17 to 25 years
6. Population — In ascending order. I for least populated district and n for highest population.

7. Area	In ascending order. I for smallest area and n for the highest
8. Contribution to the state exchequer as percentage of income of the district.	in ascending order " ,,,, ".

This methodology is adopted in the study sponsored by government of Madhya Pradesh – the only state of India to do so—— to calculate human development index at the district level.[68]

B. Taxes

1. Professional, entertainment, land revenue, cess on horticulture, minor irrigation, domestic power taxes, property, scavenging, environmental protection taxes, cottage and small scale industries, handicrafts, potable water tax, tourism, octroi etc.

In general, share in the receipt of taxes would be on the basis of subjects that are divided between the state and regions. Out of the regional share a definite part should be reserved for the sub-regional authorities like districts, block and panchayats.

2. Shared taxes: - Collection by the state minus cost of collection.

Toll tax, sales tax and excise should be shared (80 per cent for the region and 20 per cent for the state). As these taxes are collected from individuals, these should be according to the collection from that region but 20 per cent has been reserved for the state to meet the demands of equity.

3. Loans from the state government and Market:- Some of the centrally sponsored schemes which have been transferred to states and earmarked schemes may be further transferred to regions depending upon the principles of efficiency and equity. Those project benefits of which spill over across regions and are of large scale may be retained by the state but where they are of local benefit and can efficiently be handled by the regional authorities may be transferred to regions.[69]

3. Local Bodies

The share of local bodies out of the total regional revenue would be broadly on the basis of the same criteria as are being used for calculating regional share. Some of the taxes included in the regional list will be collected and retained by the local bodies. The list of such taxes would correspond to the subjects that had been allocated to the districts, blocks and panchayats. The formula for grants and shared taxes should be the same as used for calculating the share of regional authorities.

The formula further suggested that, "grants should be used on equitable and objective criteria, local bodies should be entrusted with more powers to raise funds and share revenues with higher authorities. Urban local bodies must also tap a share in rapidly rising prices of real estate".[70]

Self Rule Model of Peoples Democratic Party

The Jammu and Kashmir People's Democratic Party was founded in 1999 by the former Union Home Minister, Mufti Mohammed Sayeed. The Party contested the Assembly Election in 2002 and formed the coalition government with Congress because the party could not win majority of seats in the State Assembly. From 2002 – 2005, the Peoples Democratic Party was ruling and for another three years Congress formed the government (2005 to 2008). People's Democratic Party is presently headed by Mrs. Mehbooba Mufti while Mufti Mohammad Sayeed, who headed the PDP-Congress Coalition Government from October 2002 to November 2005, is the party's Patron.[71]

The Peoples Democratic Party's patron Mufti Mohammad Sayeed addressed a press conference near his residence in Srinagar in October, 2008, where he said that the Self-rule Document on Jammu and Kashmir is an act of hope for curbing the intraregional problem and will provide a road map for Kashmir resolution. The hope lies in the belief that if decision-makers and responsible political parties discern the categorical imperatives that have impelled this formulation and will realise its intent and motive as well as examine its contents on merits, objectively and realistically and not on partisan considerations or with chauvinistic mindset, it will be possible to forge a consensus on the way forward.[72] As such, Peoples Democratic Party has attempted an internally consistent framework and indicative direction for resolution. They have tried to contextualise the issue at various levels and drawn the contours of a process for building sustainable peace in the State and the region. The basic premises and core message of this document lies in trying to suggest a creative framework for resolution of the issue without compromising the sovereignty of the two nation states involved.[73] The Self Rule Document Reads and moves forward various proposals and measures, to address both the internal and the external dimensions of the problem in, and about Jammu and Kashmir, in a manner that is realistic and practical i.e. for the ideals of justice and empowerment for all the people of the State, for fulfilling the aspirations of the three regions and sub-regions of the State for its integrity and harmony. According to the Peoples Democratic Party's spokesperson Nayeem Akther, "This Document is an effort to find a way in the future because return to the past is not be possible - indeed, it is not even be desirable because the past offers no hope".[74]

Self Rule Document reads that, "The Jammu and Kashmir issue cannot be resolved on the basis of exclusively intra-state level initiatives. It requires a combination of intra-state measures with inter-state and supra-state measures. The approach which is underlying the concept of self-rule is a practical way that would eliminate the sources of ethno-territorial conflicts, entrenched in the traditional notions of sovereignty, self-determination, national and ethnic borders.[75] Self-rule is a formulation that will integrate the region without disturbing the extant of sovereign authority over delimited territorial space. It doesn't impair the significance of the line of control of territorial divisions but negates the acquired and imputed the manifestations of state competition for power, prestige and an imagined historical identity. It is a way of "sharing sovereignty", without the need or commitment to political merging. It is based on the creation of innovative international institutional arrangements that have political, an economic and a security character. Self Rule encompasses the society, the state, and the economy. Self Rule, being a trans-border concept, has a pan-Kashmir dimension but at the same time seeks to regionalise power across Jammu and Kashmir. Self Rule as a political philosophy is being articulated around the conception of federalism and confederation that allows the sharing of Power between two levels of the government, for the sharing of sovereignty in a coordinated but not subordinated to one another, each exercising the supreme sovereignty in its constitutional prerogatives". The comprehensive formulation of Self Rule has three subcomponents:[76]

(i) New Political Superstructure and Self Rule

The centrepiece of the governance structure under self-rule is the cross-border institution of Regional Council of Greater Jammu and Kashmir.[77] The Regional Council of Greater Jammu and Kashmir will replace the existing Upper House of State Assembly and will be a kind of a regional senate. Members of the Regional Council will be from Jammu and Kashmir as well as from Pakistan administered Kashmir. At present, the State Assembly of Jammu and Kashmir holds 20 seats for representatives from across the line of control. These will be given up and replaced by the same number of seats in the Regional Council of Greater Jammu and Kashmir.[78] This will serve as a major cross-border institution, which will ensure long-term coordination of matters and interest related to the state. Moreover, such an institutional structure will provide a framework within which certain matters between the two parts of the State and their respective mainland that needs to be sorted out to infuse in people a sense of empowerment and a feeling of belonging. This will require devising of an improved constitutional, political and economic relationship between the two parts of the State and their respective main lands. In order to empower various sub-regions within the Jammu and Kashmir state, a tier of sub-regional councils, will be added to the domestic legislative structure. While the National Parliament will have representations to the sovereign, the state assembly will continue to be a subnational institution, the sub-regional councils will complete representative character of governance by bringing in the territorial representation in the state.[79]

(ii) Economic Integration and Self Rule

Economic integration across the line of control is a very important element in the Self Rule document. As per the document, this integration can be pursued in different degrees, deepening the process as we go along and as the system and society adapts to change. The process can be started by declaring the intention to establish common economic space and sign an agreement with a roadmap which envisages:[80] Establishing a common economic space, instituting a dual currency system coordinating economic policy, harmonisation economic legislation and synergizing regulations.

The Self Rule Document suggested that the process of economic integration of the two parts of Jammu and Kashmir can start with the easiest form of economic integration, a Preferential Trade Agreement. In the Preferential Trade Agreement the two countries, India and Pakistan would offer tariff reductions, or eliminations confined to the geographical boundaries of "Greater Jammu and Kashmir" and restrict it to some product categories.[81] Stage II would be to make Greater Jammu and Kashmir (GJAK) a regional free trade area, with no tariffs or barriers between with GJAK, while maintaining their own external tariff on imports from the rest of the world, including India and Pakistan.[82] GJAK will set a common external tariff on imports from India and Pakistan. Further, instead of looking for a monetary union, a new system of "Dual Currency" would be created, where the Indian and Pakistani rupees are both made legitimate legal tenders in the geographical areas of Greater Jammu and Kashmir. A better description of this system is a "co-circulation of two currencies" in Jammu and Kashmir. It is being proposed that Indian and Pakistani rupees should be the medium of exchange in Jammu and Kashmir. To be more precise, it means, allowing circulation of the Pakistani rupee in the Indian part of Jammu and Kashmir currency and circulation of Indian rupee in the Pakistan administered Kashmir.[83] This has to be done if we want cross the Line of Control trade to flourish. Therefore, Self Rule Frame Work has focused in his economic integration part on the following point's e.g. move towards an economic union, which will maintain free trade in goods, and services, set common external tariffs, allow the free mobility of capital and labour, and will also relegate some fiscal responsibilities to a supra-national agency. However, the economic integration would be deepened through sub-regional integration; that is formation of different sub-regional groups. Again, the different sub-regional projects can generate multi-speed integration.[84] It needs to be understood that GJAK is being proposed as a regional organisation to facilitate political cooperation as well as to promote economic cooperation between India and Pakistan, and regaining Kashmir's place at the heart of Central Asia.[85]

(iii) Constitutional Restructuring and Self Rule

The constitutional restructuring is the basic spirit of self rule Document. This spirit of Self Rule Document was explained in the party meeting by Muzaffar Hussain Baig. The provisions of the constitutional restructuring were.[86]

1. "Self Rule was provided to the state in the instrument of accession but later on it was snatched and taken back from Jammu and Kashmir by the Government of India. Peopled Democratic Party now wants it to be back.
2. Even the sovereignty of the state was maintained in Delhi Agreement signed between Sheikh Mohammad Abdullah and Govt. of India. It was agreed upon that the controversial Article 356 of the Indian constitution won't be applicable to Jammu and Kashmir (by which New Delhi has powers to make legislation in place of state legislature) was as the Constitutional position stands today, Article 356, undermines the core of Self Rule and has to be made nonapplicable to Jammu and Kashmir.
3. In a similar vein, Article 249, applied to the State in amended form, should be rolled back so that the Parliament cannot exercise legislative jurisdiction over a matter that, otherwise, falls under the State jurisdiction.
4. Sixth Amendment of the Constitution of the State that undermines its original scheme of a comprehensive and accountable executive (inclusive of the Head of the State) a critical component of Self-rule will have to be repealed. Prior to this amendment, the State Legislature elected Sadar-e-Riyasat, the head of the State.
5. The proviso, limiting the powers of State Legislature, has been added to Article 368, which deals with the powers of the Parliament to amend the Constitution of India and not the power of State Legislature to amend its own Constitution. The proviso is, therefore, totally and grossly out of place and ultra virus the constitutional scheme. The State Legislature's constitutional power of amendment is the core of empowerment or Self-rule of the State and this cannot be destroyed by an order passed under Article 370. All India Service Act 1951 and Article 312 be rolled back and the local human resources are provided clear and unhindered opportunity to develop their full potential and it is trusted to manage the affairs of the State.
6. It is a part of the design of Self Rule that Head of the State be elected from the regions of Jammu and Kashmir by rotation.

This shall give to the people of all the regions an equal and equitable sense and feeling of empowerment and shall strengthen their bonds.

7. That the word 'temporary' written along with the Article 370 be deleted. At the time of accession it was envisioned that the final decision regarding accession has to be reached by the state Constituent Assembly. Later on Constituent Assembly ratified the instrument of accession, no need to have the same word 'temporary' along with Article 370".[87]

Demilitarisation and Self Rule

The proposal for demilitarisation is a very important part of the Self Rule document. According to Self Rule document, "Demilitarisation can facilitate the resolution for conceiving and debating the issue and also create an environment for the same. Because this would be the stage where mental, material and motivational reconciliation can take place on both sides of the Jammu and Kashmir state (Indian occupied Kashmir and Pak occupied Kashmir)".[88] According to the Peoples Democratic Party's spokesperson Nayeem Akther, "In the last 15 years of militancy, as experienced and observed from the last two decades, armed conflict whether on the part of militants or army and police can not bring solution to the problem. Demilitarisation has no room for armed interventions rather deliberates that the only way to solution is non-military. The demilitarisation proposal is very important to reduce not only the physical presence of the armed forces in the state but also their influence in the decision-making process, be it at the political level or the administrative level. Even at the operational matters of security, the armed forces should be a part of the Jammu and Kashmir police hierarchy rather than being a parallel institution of power. The whole change in the form of demilitarisation is being proposed by Peoples Democratic Party as the demilitarisation model".[89] He further said that the simple fact of withdrawal of troops is indicative of the preconditions for resolution and resolution oriented measures. It symbolises a conceptual change in governance by the government; a growing leadership confidence in the state, and a politically courageous pro-active leadership at the national level. Since 2000, the balance of power on governing was in favour of civil institutions, lead to a situation where the democratic and civil society institutions are given full charge of the situation to consolidate the peace process. But the withdrawal of troops should be pragmatic and objective i.e. it should be only from civilian areas. It will create and enhance the situation for peace process of the people of Jammu and Kashmir themselves.[90] Moreover, Demilitarisation process will create positive impact on the ground at the Line of Control and state level; it also has national and international ramifications. The former strengthens the claim and later the case. The demilitarisation process also focuses on the Armed Forces Special Powers Act (AFSPA) which is still in force from the last two decades.[91] There is no justification for this to operate any further and must be repealed to enable normalisation to take roots. The most important fall out of this will be that it will empower and facilitate state government in assuming its full role in revitalising and pushing forward the control of civil society over the governance of the state.[92] Therefore, the struggle for repeal of this Lawless of the Law (AFSPA) and demilitarisation to be intensified is also necessary for the protection of human rights".[93]

Autonomy and Self Rule

National Conference passed a greater autonomy resolution in 1994 and later on National Conference got a resolution on similar lines passed by Jammu and Kashmir Assembly in 2000. Some termed the Greater Autonomy model of National Conference as moving to pre-1953 position before the arrest of Sheikh Abdullah in August 1953. National Conference did not directly say so but it was surely something like that. On the other hand, People's Democratic Party patron Mufti Mohammed Sayeed, has the National Conference as the first rival party, had to come up before the people of Jammu and Kashmir with something that looked different or more than the Greater Autonomy of National Conference.[94] Ultimately, Peoples Democratic Party came up with self rule model which addresses the problem of Jammu and Kashmir in four different dimensions, which includes New Delhi-state relations; relations between the two divided parts of Jammu and Kashmir, resource sharing including trade, transport and other issues; relations between Pakistan and Pakistan occupied Kashmir (POK) and the document focuses also on inter-regional and sub-regional issues like, the currencies of both India and Pakistan should be used in Jammu and Kashmir and POK and there should be common control of India and Pakistan on certain subjects as would pertain to Jammu and Kashmir and POK.[95]

The President of People's Democratic Party Mehbooba Mufti has defined the PDP's Self Rule document within the scope of 1947 instrument of accession and the constitution of India. To remain in political race and lay hands on the seat of governance it has to make its stand on 1947 accession of Jammu and Kashmir with India so that New Delhi does not go against the policies of Peoples Democratic Party. On 9th July 2009, in a special meeting presided over by Mehbooba Mufti said,

1. "Our Self Rule document is different from National Conference's greater autonomy because the document encompasses the society, the state and the economy. It comprises a nexus of multiple loyalties of an individual as a member of the society, duties and rights of the citizen in a reciprocal political arrangement with the state and the role of the individual as a producer and consumer in the economy.
2. Self Rule refers to autonomy from the nation state of India where as autonomy connotes relative autonomy from the Government of India.
3. Autonomy refers to empowerment of the government of Jammu and Kashmir vis-à-vis the government of India. As such, it becomes a part of the centre-state debate in the Indian federal set up. Self Rule on the other hand refers to the empowerment of the people of Jammu and Kashmir vis–à-vis the nation of India.
4. Self Rule has four separate components; autonomy, control, legitimacy and identity. Autonomy refers to the independence of a state in making policies. Control refers to the actual ability of the state to produce the outcomes it desires. Legitimacy refers to its process through which the people in power have reached that position. Identity refers to the capacity of the state to endow people with an overriding sense of who they are as a collective group.
5. Self Rule as political philosophy can be articulated around the conception of federation and confederation that allow for sharing of power, between two levels of government for the sharing of sovereignty in a coordinated but not subordinate to one another, each exercising supreme sovereignty in its

> constitutional prerogatives. When Indian Independence Act was passed and the two dominions of India and Pakistan came into being, Jammu and Kashmir became an independent country. It is for that reason that Jammu and Kashmir fell in the category of fully empowered Indian states. It is this sovereign status of the ruler of the state that is supposed to provide legal foundation to the instrument of accession with the dominion of India".[96]

By and large Peoples Democratic Party is nearly echoing what National Conference has been demanding. National Conference did ask for Greater Autonomy but never fought for a mass movement to attain the same. National Conference did not do much work to carry the message of Greater Autonomy to ground level masses, particularly in Jammu and Ladakh regions. The similar status and position in both the parties is that they have accepted the 1947 accession of Jammu and Kashmir with India.[97]

Chenab Formula Model

In 1960, the Prime Minister of Azad Kashmir Sardar Hayat Khan, outlined the Chenab Formula as the most preferred option to solve the long pending Kashmir issue along the river Chenab. Under this proposal, "India would retain Hindu and Buddhist majority areas of Jammu and Ladakh while Northern Areas, Pakistan Occupied Kashmir (POK), Kashmir valley and districts of Muslim majority in Jammu and Kargil regions would join Pakistan".[98] This formula is actually based on the 'Dixon Plan', proposed in 1950 by Sir Owen Dixon, who came as a United Nation's Representative for India and Pakistan; assigned Ladakh to India, the Gilgit - Baltistan and Pakistan occupied Kashmir to Pakistan, split Jammu between the two and envisaged a plebiscite in the Kashmir valley".[99] The river Chenab comes out from Himalayan range of Kullus in the extreme north of Kishtwar in Doda district (Jammu province) with high mountain range of Himachal (India) adjoining in the background. It flows through the mountainous areas of Doda, Ramban, Surankot, Salat, Reasi and Akhnoor and enters into Punjab (Pakistan) at Head Marala where a big headwork has been built facilitating construction of two big channels. India has built Salal dam on it under Indus Water Treaty. On the right bank of Chenab river, is lingering half of mountainous Doda district, the entire Gulab Garh tehsil of Udhampur district, at a very long distance fall the districts of Rajouri and Poonch, all being the Muslim majority areas contiguously linked with Kashmir province, which had six districts at that time (presently Jammu and Kashmir constitutes twenty two Districts, ten districts from Jammu, ten districts from Kashmir Valley and two districts from Ladakh region) with majority of Muslim population. On the left bank of Chenab fall, the Tehsils of Bhadarwah, Kishtwar having Muslim majority population, and at extreme start the districts of Udhampur, Jammu and Kathua with Hindu majority.[100]

The Chenab Formula seeks to divide Kashmir along the river Chenab, which flows down from Kashmir into Punjab (Pakistan), separating the Muslim-majority areas from the Hindu and Buddhist-dominated ones. According to Chenab formula, "Out of six districts of Jammu province almost three districts fall on the right bank of Chenab River having close contiguity with Kashmir province. Only three districts with majority Hindu population fall on the left bank of the river. According to M. Reddy, "Chenab division of division of Jammu and Kashmir, eighty- per cent territory of the state including Azad Kashmir and Northern areas becomes part of Pakistan while only twenty per cent is being left with India.[101] This kind of solution of Jammu and Kashmir could be a windfall for Pakistan".[102] As per this formula, the city of Jammu and some districts of Jammu province would go to India, while the city of Srinagar and most parts of the Kashmir valley as well as parts of Jammu region would be transferred to Pakistan. This division would be based on the flow of the Chenab, but it would to some extent coincide with religious demography.[103] However, the Pakistan's interest in the Chenab formula is only Kashmir being a part of Pakistan, and entire Jammu province and Ladakh under India. One evident outcome of such an arrangement would be the dissolving of the Indus Waters Treaty, as the political status of Kashmir would change. The distribution of water resources would be altered. Pakistan would then have complete control over only the Indus, Jhelum, and some of their tributaries. The Chenab, Ravi, Beas and Sutlej rivers would fall under India's jurisdiction. This arrangement would be detrimental to Pakistan, as it would lose a major water source, 'the Chenab'. This implies a thirty billion cubic meter or seventeen per cent reduction in water flows in the Indus System in Pakistan, provided, of course, that India is able to block the Chenab completely.[104] The incumbent major water resources for Pakistan, Indus and Jhelum have already been exploited to the maximum in Pakistani Punjab itself where over half of their water flows, is diverted for irrigation. The Chenab also is a major source of water to Punjab. Moreover, the Chenab-Jhelum combine is the only tributary of the Indus that enhances the latter's flood downstream Punjab. Losing Chenab to India would mean drastic reduction in water supplies to Sindh, which is already on the brink of a water crisis. It is imperative to note here that the location where the eastern tributaries merge to join the Indus River is at a point just prior to entering Sindh. Moreover, Sindh receives water only from the Indus River. Losing Chenab would also warrant a major rearrangement of the irrigation network in Punjab. This clearly explains Pakistan's insistence on making Chenab the basis of the international border and including parts of Jammu and not merely the Kashmir valley, under its jurisdiction. Furthermore, accepting the Chenab Formula implies that India would have to part with approximately 32,000 sq km of area, which includes the districts of Anantnag, Baramulla, Budgam, Doda, Kupwara, Pulwama, Poonch, Rajouri, Srinagar, and the Gool Gulabgarh and Reasi Tehsils of Udhampur that is giving away fifty per cent of the total land area of Jammu & Kashmir, excluding Ladakh and the area under China and Pakistan. An interesting aspect of Pakistan's claim over these districts is that the catchment areas of all the rivers important to Pakistan Indus, Jhelum and Chenab would come under Pakistan's jurisdiction.[105]

Robert Wirsing writes, "The physical control over the Chenab valley is being sought, as it would help Pakistan to build dams upstream and regulate the river flows to Punjab and Sindh. Moreover, it provides strategic depth for the Mangla Dam and the Pothohar region. While Mangla Dam is an exclusive Dam for Punjab, Pothohar provides the Pakistani army with more than half of its recruits. However, this proposition is a zero-sum game from the perspective of Indian security. Foremost, India would have to part with the strategically vital Akhnoor area in Jammu, which is the only all-weather route available to India. To the south of Akhnoor lies the 'Chicken's Neck' a narrow strip of Pakistani territory.[106] It is interesting to note that during the Indo-Pak wars of 1965 and 1971, Pakistan had launched attacks to capture Akhnoor and the strategic bridge across the Chenab, which clearly highlights Akhnoor's significance".[107] The Akhnoor Bridge is currently

India's sole link to Poonch valley. Besides, the area around Akhnoor is of primary strategic importance as it provides the best terrain for inter-border movement and is most conducive for large-scale operations. Ladakh's accessibility will be compromised, with India turning dependent on Pakistan to access supply routes to Ladakh. Thus, based purely on military considerations, India cannot accept Chenab as the basis of the new international border. Moreover, losing Chenab would not bode well for parts of Jammu the districts of Jammu, Kathua, Kargil and parts of Udhampur that would remain with India.[108]

Kashmir in Chenab Formula

M. Reddy while analysing the Chenab Formula writes, "The Chenab Formula appears to be Pakistan's desired solution to the Kashmir issue. Acquiring the territory of Kashmir, including parts of Jammu, can provide Pakistan with the opportunity to tap rivers in the present Indian Kashmir. Storage facilities that it is unable to develop within its own territory can then be constructed in Kashmir. A major benefit of tapping the rivers would be the increased hydropower generation, which to a great extent can help electrify Kashmir under its jurisdiction, as well as regulate supplies to Punjab. The construction of canals and water courses can also bring better irrigation to Kashmir, and regulate water flows to Punjab".[109] However, a caveat to this proposal cannot be overlooked. Once Pakistan takes control of Kashmir as another federating unit of the country, its development needs and demands will have to be on par with the other provinces in the country. Bringing it into the mainstream will entail a cost in terms of pumping in funds and at the same time attracting investments, for developing the water resources of the region. However, once irrigation canals are constructed, Kashmir being an agricultural region, it will begin demanding its share of waters. This would imply having another contending recipient to the already controversial water sharing formula.[110] Further, diverting waters to irrigate Kashmir's lands would mean reducing flows to Punjab and Sindh, which will never be acceptable to the two leading provinces of the country[111].

Moreover, Sindh, which is already suffering the consequences of reduced water flows, will witness a further decline and erosion of its economy. This will add another dimension to the protracted water dispute in Pakistan with Punjab and Sindh joining hands to resist

Kashmir.[112] Under such circumstances, Pakistan will be caught in a perennial web of provincial disharmony. By this, clearly it will be in Pakistan's interest to not make Kashmir another federating unit of Pakistan, but rather have it as an 'independent' state sub-let to Pakistan.[113] Thus, the option of controlling only the Vale of Kashmir is futile for Pakistan, while the Chenab Formula is an invitation to war with India. The option of the Chenab formula benefits Pakistan, but it inflicts heavy costs on the people of Jammu & Kashmir and security costs on India. The option of the Vale as the Base is destructive for both India and Pakistan.[114]

Ladakh Autonomous Hill Development Council Model

Ladakh's perception about its place in Jammu and Kashmir has its genesis in an age old political contradictions. The state formed in March 1846 under the Treaty of Amritsar between the British and Jammu ruler Gulab Singh, was devoid of any geo-political character. Many people in Ladakh, including Shias of Kargil and Baltistan, showed dismay over the irretrievable merger of their identity with Jammu and Kashmir.[115] Frederich Drew who served as governor in Ladakh in the nineteenth century remarked, "The territories of Jammu and Kashmir have no other bond of cohesion than the fact of Maharaja's rule, no simple name for it exists".[116]

In fact, Ladakh had no case, at the time of independence movement, to put forward its view except that its people felt emotionally and spiritually closer to Tibet. Nonetheless, the sole organisation in the region, the Ladakh Buddhist Association (LBA), was actively guided by a few Kashmiri pundits to put forward a case for separating Ladakh from Jammu and Kashmir in favour of an administrative solution within the Indian system.[117]

A memorandum to Maharaja Hari Singh and the Prime Minister of India on May 4, 1949, by Cheewang Rigzin, President, Ladakh Buddhist Association, opposed the proposed plebiscite and demanded that Ladakh be governed either by the Maharaja without tagging it on to Kashmir, amalgamated with Jammu to form a separate province or be permitted to join East Punjab. The memorandum underlined the strategic and commercial importance of neighbouring Tibet and China, with Leh as the new centre of the Central Asian Trade. But neither Maharaja Hari Singh nor Jawaharlal Nehru responded to the appeal.[118]

Thus, Ladakh's maladjustment with Jammu and Kashmir started from the very beginning. According to Ladakh Buddhist Association, "Clearly the Kashmiri leadership had no interest in Ladakh. They enjoyed a free hand in exercising sabre–rattling and jingoism towards the region's Buddhist heritage. They were also annoyed with the "step–motherly treatment" meted out to Ladakh in the allocation of funds. No doubt the centre earmarks funds for the development of Ladakh, but the people and politicians of Ladakh allege that officers and engineers of Kashmiri origin "pocket" most of these funds with the result that only a fraction of the central funds are utilised for development projects".[119] In fact, every Enquiry Commission, including the Gajendragadkar Commission (1967-68), the Sikri Commission (1979-80), the Wazir Commission (1982-83) and the Singhal Committee (1998) have invariably acknowledged an unambiguous language that the ruling class has all along treated Ladakh shabbily[120]. The Commissions cited innumerable instances of discrimination and the valley's apathy vis–à–vis Ladakh.[121] Thus, repeated agitations by the Buddhists of Ladakh continued for separating it from Kashmir were quelled by using force. The protests ranged from the demand for "Greater Autonomy" in the 1950's, "North Eastern Federation Association type" administration in the 1960's, "central administration" in the 1970's, "free Ladakh from Kashmir in the 1980's and the demand for "union territory status" in the 1990's.[122]

A violent struggle launched by Ladakh Buddhist Association (LBA), in 1989, giving a call to free Ladakh from Kashmir could be brought under the control only after a tripartite agreement among the representatives of the Ladakh Buddhist Association (LBA), the state government and the central government was signed in October 1989, the Ladakh Buddhist Association (LBA) agreed to compromise: it would withdraw the demand for union territory status in return for the establishment of an Autonomous Hill Council, along the lines of the Darjeeling Gorkha Hill Council. This arrangement would provide a mechanism for self-governance, local autonomy in administration, economy and planning.[123] However, through out the 1990's Ladakh remained bogged down with its own affairs, such as the non-implementation of the provisions stated in the tripartite agreement? According to Ladakh Buddhist Association, Farooq Abdullah's government was the main hurdle in the non-implementation of the provisions. Finally, in order to meet the regional grievances of Ladakh especially the demand for Autonomous Hill Council, in October, 1993, the Union Government and State Government agreed to get Ladakh the status of Autonomous Council.[124] Thus, Ladakh Autonomous Hill Development Council (LAHDC) was created in 1995 under the Act of Ladakh Autonomous Hill Development Council (LAHDC) Act as a regional autonomous model following the demands of Ladakhi People to make the district a new union territory because of its religious differences with Kashmir.[125] This Act consists of ten chapters and describe in detail regarding the constitution of Ladakh Autonomous Hill Development Council, its territorial constituencies, election to the council, oath of affirmation by members etc. in first two chapters, the total number of seats in the LAHDC elected on the basis of adult franchise will be twenty six (26). The Governor has been empowered to nominate four members to the council from among the principal minority and women in the district to the members of the Council. The chapter third is related with the powers and functions of the Council while fourth deals with conduct of the business of the Council. Chapter fifth deals with the Executive Council, its composition, powers and functions etc. Chapter sixth deals with the officers and servants of the Council including Chief Executive Officer and Secretary. Chapter seven, deals with the transfer of land to the Council. While Chapter eight deals with the funds and audit of the council. Chapter ninth deals the constitution of inter-district advisory council and chapter tenth deals with the miscellaneous power of council, power to issue direction, dissolution of the council, power to make rules and regulations.[126]

Formal Structure and Electoral Policy of the Council

After the establishment of Ladakh Autonomous Hill Council, the elections were held, and the first Hill Council (for Leh) was sworn in on September 3, 1995. There are thirty seats in the council, twenty-six of which are filled by people chosen directly on the basis of adult suffrage from territorial constituencies. The remaining four seats are filled by people nominated directly by the Governor of the State from among the principal minorities (i.e. Muslims) and women in the district. Constituency boundaries were drawn in collaboration between state officials and local leaders so as to ensure adequate representation from sparsely populated regions of the district, and to prevent domination by central Ladakh (Leh and surrounding areas in the Indus valley). Members of the council meet at least once a year, and elect from among themselves a Chief Executive Councillor, who in turn chooses from among the council members four Executive Councillors. These five constitute the daily executive body of the Council. One of the four executive councillors is being chosen from among the principal minorities.[127]

Powers and Functions of the Council

The powers and function of the council is to give allotment, use and occupation of land vested in the council, formulation and review of progress of development programmes for the district, formulation of the Budget for the district, formulation of guidelines for implementation of schemes at the grassroot level, promotion of languages and culture of the area, management of un-demarcated forests, management of canals or water courses for agriculture, desert development, tourism planning, promotion, and development, vocational training, preservation of the environment and ecology of the area.[128] The Council has also, extensive rights to levy and collect local taxes and fees of all sorts, including on grazing, business, transport, entertainment, temporary occupation of village sites, roads, etc. The Council has the power to hire and fire almost all levels of public servants, and all government employees, with the exception of judiciary and police personnel, who could be 'transferred' to the Council but at the discretion of the government to recall them.[129]

Hill Council, Autonomy and Community

Hari Om writes, "While analyzing the autonomous character of Hill Council and its role vis-à-vis the development of community character, it is important here to see the operational side of the Hill Council. While there is no doubt that the Hill Development Act and the institution of the Council in Leh constitutes an important change in the Indian and State government's centralised top down approach to development planning and implementation. But one still needs to ask who is being empowered in Ladakh, on what basis and to what extent. For this, here are some important issues for the same. First, all plans and budgets that the Council may draw up still require approval from the State government and in any case are constrained as they are to be formulated within the priorities and broad principles contained in National and State Five Year Plans, etc.[130] Second, most funds still flow through the Kashmir Government. In the past, the late release of funds by the State has made it impossible for the Ladakhi administration to carry out programmes. Third, there are important party political uncertainties and dependencies that compromise the powers of the Council. While the Congress party in 1996 bagged all seats on the council, the new popularly elected government in Kashmir has been formed by the National Conference, old supporters of Congress at the Leh District level".[131] The Chief Minister Farooq Abdullah, has appointed National Conference members from Ladakh to important positions in his administration, effectively sidelining the Hill Council and Congress. Already voices are heard in Leh that threaten to resume an agitation for total secession from the State which was the original demand in 1989, 'free Ladakh from Kashmir'.[132] Apart from these supra-local concerns and constraints, there are local problems with representation and participation in the Council too. First, in spite of the attempts to ensure that local people represent constituencies, in practice even remote constituencies are represented through people based in Leh; this Leh dominance has been a cause of resentment and hence loss of legitimacy of the council. Second, and more seriously perhaps, autonomy was achieved through an agitation that created rather than reflected a fundamental division of Ladakh's population into Buddhists and Muslims.[133] While the formal structure of the Council takes this polarisation into account and ensures representation on the Council for the Muslims, it on the one hand institutionalises this 'communalisation', and on the other ignores other important divisions and 'communities' that are irreducible to geographic or religious 'communities'.[134] In short, while constituencies seek to address geographical differences assuming congruence of location and community, and the special provisions in the Act seek to address religious differences assuming congruence of religion and community, other important differences which we may not recognise as 'communities', e.g. based on occupation, gender, age, class, to name a few are not or barely addressed at all.[135]

The Issue of Development and Council

There is an implicit and sometimes explicit assumption that empowerment of local communities especially those deemed traditional will lead to better- locally, socially, culturally, environmentally appropriate development planning and practice. This assumption is premised on the same unproblematic understanding of 'local community', 'tradition' and 'interest' as the legal/institutional principles of the Hill Council formula.[136] The Hill Council was created in order to meet a demand for local (district) autonomy, for a stronger voice of people in Ladakh in decision-making, planning and implementation of 'development'. The specific grievances, as expressed in memoranda and other submissions, that gave rise to the demand however are not so much criticisms of the goals or course of existing Government's development efforts, but 'merely' of its pace too slow, its distribution privileging of other parts of the State and/or other religious communities, and its 'size' more money should be allocated for Ladakh, because the region is so huge and sparsely populated.[137] The criticism, then, does not reflect any critique of 'conventional' development, nor does it put much emphasis on environmental or cultural protection. At the same time, the justification for devolution of power to Ladakh is made especially in terms of cultural and environmental difference. Apparently, at least in this case, there is an important difference between demands and their justifications and consequently in the policies and priorities of the Council. Since public political discourse and practice, including the Council, is dominated by members of the new economic elite which to some extent converges with the old aristocracy. There has been rather little in the way of more sustainable (however defined) development policies. Immediate concerns of the local political and economic elite centre about continued exemption from taxes, expansion of flights to Leh, improvement of roads etc., all with a view to promoting trade. While the executive council seeks to make agriculture and other 'traditional' livelihoods more attractive, this is very much connected to the individuals on top of the executive council, two of whom used to run the Ladakh Ecological Development.[138] Since the installation of the Council, they have been under sustained attack from practically all sides, including their own former supporters within the communalised Ladakh Buddhist Association. There is no agreement locally on the direction and kind of development that is deemed desirable or appropriate for Ladakh, and in fact the dominant voices are those of proponents of more and faster economic development along the same old path. Former politics and administration is still mostly a game of men in Central Ladakh of the modern educated, salaried, and urban population.[139] The growing radical resistance against the old and new political elites including the Ecological Development elite is carried primarily by the unemployed or underemployed and educated youth.

They do not generally want sustainable development, a healthy environment or culture, but jobs. They want Ladakh to be more like Delhi in terms of bright lights and 'facilities'. There are a number of shifting alliances between these radical youths, the Buddhist 'fundamentalists' and their Muslim counterparts, the National Conference and Congress and the religious and aristocratic 'traditional' elites. These forces, complex and irreducible to any simple community, dominate the politics in Ladakh. The Hill Council, as Y. R. Sharma, argued, has not resolved this problem, but exacerbated it. The villagers, farmers, nomads, are largely kept out from these processes, because for their 'communities'. There is no voice in the formal structure of the Hill Council.[140] He further says, neither geographical constituency nor religious community representation can really address the varied aspirations, multiple forms of demands, in which 'community' is established, practiced, challenged and used. The attempt to empower the 'local people' in Ladakh has been based on the logic of fragmentation that has created new divisions and institutionalised others, thus changing the meaning of community and belonging altogether. Many, if not most, common sense conceptions of empowerment of local communities tend to assume an unproblematic convergence of livelihood, location, identification and interest. In practice, unfortunately, such simple sociality is rarely if ever present in people's lives, their understanding of themselves and others.[141] The mere institutional or legal 'empowerment' of local communities does not address in itself issues of social justice and inequality and certainly does not lead naturally or necessarily to 'better' policies for mountains and their populations. At the same time, of course, devolution and decentralisation are the indispensable component of any attempt to move towards social justice and sustainability. The challenge is to reconceptualise community representation and the institutional arrangements we envision, so that we do not close our eyes to the issues of inequality and social justice nor foster divisions among 'communities' that we wish to exist".[142]

Notes

1. Ghai, Yash (ed.), *Ethnicity and Autonomy: A frame work for Analysis, in autonomy and ethnicity*, Ghai Pub. Cambridge University Press, p. 8.
2. Sisk Timothy, D. *Power sharing and international mediation in ethnic conflicts*, United States Institute of Peace, Washington, D.C. 1996, p. 5.

3. Wirsing Robert, G. *Kashmir in the shadows of war, Regional Rivalries in a Nuclear* Age, Pub. M.E. Sharpe, New York, 2002, p. 197.
4. Lapidoth, Ruth, *Autonomy, Flexible Solutions to ethnic Conflicts,* (Washington, D.C; United States Institute of Peace, 1996), p. 33.
5. *Ibid;* p. 53.
6. Wirsing Robert, G. *Kashmir in the shadows of war, Regional Rivalries in a Nuclear Age,* Pub. M. E. Sharpe, New York, 2002, p.199.
7. Gurr Ted, Robert, *Ethnic warfare on the wane*, Foreign Affairs (May/ June 2000) pp. 52-64.
8. Sisk, Timothy D. *Power sharing and international mediation in ethnic conflicts*, (Washington, D. C; United States Institute of Peace, 1996), p. 106.
9. Bonedikter, Thomas, *Territorial Autonomy: A Solution for open Ethnic Conflicts*, Foreign Affairs (March 20, 2008) p. 100.
10. Prof. Rehmatullah, *Regional Autonomy Experiments in other countries* in Puri Balraj, *Regional Autonomy Report (J&K) in 1999*, Jay Kay Publishers, p. 73.
11. *Ibid;* pp. 75-80.
12. Samaddar, Ranabir (ed.), *The Politics of Autonomy Indian Experience,* Sage Publication, New Delhi, 2005, p. 19.
13. Basu, D.D. *Introduction to The Constitution of India*, 19th edition 2007, Wadhwa and company law publishers, New Delhi, pp. 273-77.
14. Samaddar, Ranabir, (ed.), *The Politics of Autonomy Indian Experience* Sage Publication, New Delhi, 2005, pp. 19-20.
15. Om, Hari and Rekha Chowdhery (eds.), *Politics of Autonomy in Jammu and Kashmir,* p. 187.
16. Mandla, Sunita, *The Politics of state Autonomy and Regional Identity*, Manohar publishers, New Delhi, 1992, p. 178.
17. M. L. Gopta, *Kashmir: A Wailing Valley*, Anmol Publications, New Delhi, 2001, pp. 139-40.
18. Kak, Shakti, *Hindutva*, *The Crisis of the state and political mobilisation in Jammu and Kashmir, Contemporary perspectives of History and Sociology*, Vol. 3, No. 1, Jan – June 2009, Cambridge University Press – India Pvt. Ltd pp. 14-33.
19. Puri Balraj, *Simmering Volcano, study of Jammu's relation with Kashmir*, Sterling Publishers Pvt Limited, 1983, p. 35.
20. Puri, Balraj, *How Government Scuttled Regional Autonomy*, Economic and Political Weekly, June 5, 1999, p. 1400.
21. *Regional Autonomy Committee Report Govt. of Jammu and Kashmir*, 1999, p. 2.
22. *Ibid;* p. 3.
23. Behera, N.C. *Demystifying Kashmir*, Pub, Dorling Kindersley (India) Delhi, 2007, pp. 133-134.

24. Kaur, Ravinderjit, *Why Autonomy to Kashmir*, Institute of Peace and Conflict Studies, September 2003.
25. *Ibid.*
26. *Ibid.*
27. Wirsing Robert, G. *Regional Rivalries in a Nuclear Age*, Pub. M.E. Shale Armonk, New York London – England, p. 205.
28. *The Report of Regional Autonomy Committee Report 1999 Govt. of Jammu and Kashmir.*
29. Kamraz (*Baramulla and Kupwara Districts*) Nundabad *(Budgam and Srinagar Districts*) Maraz (*Anantnag and Pulwama Districts*) Chenab valley (*Doda District and Tehsile Mahore*) Jammu (*Jammu, Kathua and Udhampur excluding district Mahore*) Pir Panchal (*Poonch and Rajouri Districts*) Ladakh (*Leh District*), Kargil (*Kargil District*).
30. *Regional Autonomy Committee Report Government of Jammu and Kashmir 1999.*
31. *Nund Abad region* constitutes the Budgam and Srinagar Districts of the Kashmir Province.
32. *Maraz* is the South side of the valley of Kashmir, consisting of District Anantnag, Kulgam, Shopian and District Pulwama.
33. Kashmir Times, April 27, 1999.
34. Greater Kashmir, July 19, 2000.
35. Behera, N. C. *Demystifying Kashmir*, Pub. Dorling Kindersley (India) Delhi, 2007, p. 135.
36. Kashmir Times, April 21, 1999.
37. Greater Kashmir, 21st September 2000.
38. *Regional Autonomy Committee report Government of Jammu and Kashmir*, 1999, p. 8.
39. Kishtwari, Aseer, *Focus on Jammu and Kashmir*, Crescent Publications, Jammu, 2006, p. 556.
40. *Regional Autonomy Committee report Government of Jammu and Kashmir*, 1999, p. 8.
41. Ganguly, Sumit, *The Kashmir Question Retrospect and Prospect*, Frank CASS Great Britain, 2003, pp. 17-18.
42. Greater Kashmir, 24 June 2000.
43. Habibullah Wajahat, *My Kashmir Conflict and the prospects of enduring peace*, United States institute of peace, 2008, pp. 154-155.
44. *Regional Autonomy Committee report Government of Jammu and Kashmir*, 1999, p. 8.
45. *Kashmir Times*, 5, May 1999.
46. Puri, Balraj, *Jammu and Kashmir Regional Autonomy: A Report,* Jay Kay Publishing House, Jammu, pp. Xiii.

47. Puri, Balraj, *Kashmir: Towards Insurgency*, Pub. Orient Longman Limited, New Delhi, 1995, p. 29.
48. *Ibid.*, pp. 29-30.
49. Puri, Balraj, *Jammu and Kashmir Regional Autonomy*: A Report, pp. xii-xiii.
50. *Human Rights journal*, issue, July – August, 2002, p. 4.
51. Puri, Balraj, *Jammu and Kashmir Regional Autonomy*: A Report.
52. *Report of Jammu and Kashmir Commission of Inquiry*, Government of Jammu and Kashmir, December, 1968, p. 83.
53. Puri, Balraj, *The Autonomy Debate, Frontline Magazine* March 2003, pp. 18-31, and Jammu on the Brink, Hindu, 21 August, 2001.
54. Habibullah Wajahat, *My Kashmir Conflict and the prospects of enduring peace*, United States Institute of Peace, 2008, pp. 154-155.
55. Ganguly, Sumit, *The Kashmir Question Retrospect and Prospect*, Frank CASS, Great Britan, 2003, pp. 17-18.
56. Puri, Balraj, *Jammu and Kashmir Regional Autonomy: A Report*, Jay Kay Publishing House, Jammu, p. 19.
57. Wirsing Robert, G. *Kashmir in the shadows of war, Regional Rivalries in a Nuclear Age*, Pub. M.E. Sharpe, New York, 2002, p. 205.
58. Kumar, Ashutosh, *Some thoughts on the debate on Autonomy in Jammu and Kashmir*, Mainstream December 23, 2000, p. 74.
59. Saxena, Ashish, *Reflections on Democratic Decentralisation in Jammu and Kashmir*, Economic and Political Weekly Magazine, March 1, 2008.
60. Puri, Balraj, *Jammu and Kashmir Regional Autonomy: A Report,* Jay Kay Publishing House, Jammu, p. 21.
61. *Ibid;* pp. 21-22.
62. Lapidoth Ruth, *Cultural Autonomy: Flexible Solutions to Ethnic Conflicts*, United States Institute of Peace, Washington, D.C. 1996, p. 33.
63. Puri, Balraj, *Jammu and Kashmir Regional Autonomy: A Report*, Jay Kay Publishing House, Jammu, pp. 27-28.
64. *Ibid;* p. 31.
65. Puri, Balraj, *The evolution of Indian Federalism: Strengths and Weakness,* in Jain L.C. *Decentralisation and local governance*, (ed.), Orient Longman New Delhi, 2005, pp. 97-98.
66. *Human Development Report forward 1995*, p. 111.
67. Puri' Balraj, *Jammu and Kashmir Regional Autonomy: A Report*, Jay Kay Publishing House, Jammu, pp. 27-28.
68. Madhya Pradesh Human Development Report 1995.
69. Puri, Balraj, *Jammu and Kashmir Regional Autonomy: A* Report, Jay Kay Publishing House, Jammu, pp. 44-45.
70. Puri, Balraj, *The evolution of Indian Federalism: Strengths and Weakness, Decentralisation and local government*, p. 96.

71. http://en.wikipedia.org/wiki/Jammu_and_Kashmir_People's_Democratic_ Party.
72. Syed Bashrat, Mufti Finally Unveils PDP's Self Rule, Kashmir Times, Sunday 26th October,
73. Kashmir Times, 28th October, 2008.
74. Interview with Naeem Akther, Dated 12th Feb. 2011.
75. Greater Kashmir, October 26, 2008.
76. *Self Rule Frame Work: A Way Forward*, http://www.jkpdp.org/.
77. Greater Jammu and Kashmir includes both the Indian occupied Kashmir and the Pak occupied Kashmir.
78. Kashmir Times, October 28, 2008.
79. Bukhari, Shujaat, *PDP unveils Self Rule framework for Kashmir,* The Hindu, October, 26, 2008.
80. *Self Rule Frame Work: A Way Forward*, http://www.jkpdp.org/.
81. Greater Kashmir, 27 October, 2008.
82. Kashmir Times, November 11, 2008.
83. Sagar, Daya, *Greater Autonomy or Self Rule; what difference does it make*, Kashmir Times, November 7, 2009.
84. Sayeed Mohd. Malik, *More than autonomy but less than a viable road map*, Kashmir Times, November 10, 2008.
85. Kashmir Times, October 20, 2008.
86. Sagar Daya, *Greater Autonomy or Self Rule; what difference does it make*, Kashmir Times, November 7, 2009.
87. *Self Rule Frame Work: A Way Forward*, http://www.jkpdp.org/.
88. Kashmir Times, October 26, 2008.
89. Interview with Naeem Akhter, Dated 12th Feb. 2011.
90. Greater Kashmir, October 28, 2008.
91. Kashmir Times, November 20, 2009.
92. *Self Rule Frame Work: A Way Forward,* http://www.jkpdp.org/.
93. Interview with Naeem Akhter, Dated 12th Feb. 2011.
94. Sagar, Daya, *Greater Autonomy or Self Rule; What difference does it make,* Kashmir Times, November 7, 2009.
95. Greater Kashmir, October, 26, 2008.
96. *Self Rule Frame Work: A Way Forward,* http://www.jkpdp.org/.
97. Sagar, Daya, *Greater Autonomy or Self Rule; what difference does it make,* Kashmir Times, November 7, 2009.
98. Pugwash consultation on the Kashmir issue, A chronology of negotiations and CBMs between India and Pakistan 23 April 2005, Srinagar.
99. Sehbai, Shaheen, *Mushraf Convinced Chenab Formula, the Only Acceptable Solution of Kashmir*, South Asia Tribune, March 10 2005.

100. Ahmed, Khaled, *Second opinion: What is the Chenab Formula*? The Daily Times, 3 July 2003.
101. Reddy, B. Muralidhar, *The Mushraf Formula*, Frontline, Vol. 21. Issue 23, November 06-19- 2004.
102. *Ibid.*
103. Ahmed, Khaled, *Second opinion: What is the Chenab Formula?* The Daily Times, 3 July 2003.
104. Wirsing Robert, G. and Christopher Jasparro, Robert G. *River Diplomacy: India, Pakistan, And The Baglihar Dam Dispute*, Asia-Pacific Center for Security Studies, May 2000.
105. Shah, Farzana, *Chenab Formula,* Pakistan Times, Tuesday September 23, 2008.
106. www.strategicforesight.com/finalsettlement/chp9options.pdf.
107. Wirsing Robert, G. and Christopher Jasparro, Robert G. *River Diplomacy: India, Pakistan, And The Baglihar Dam Dispute*, Asia-Pacific Center for Security Studies, May 2000.
108. *Ibid.*
109. Reddy, B. Muralidhar, *The Mushraf Formula*, Frontline, Vol. 21. Issue 23, November. 06-19, 2004.
110. Iyer, R. R, *Indus Treaty: A Different View, Economic and Political Weekly*, Vol. 11, n. 29 (16 July 2005), p. 3144.
111. *Ibid;* pp. 314-315.
112. *Ibid;* pp. 314-315.
113. Waslekar, S. *The Final Settlement: Restructuring India-Pakistan Relations* (Mumbai: Strategic Foresight Group, 2005), p. 58.
114. Singh, Madanjeet, *South Asian agenda for Jammu & Kashmir*, The Hindu, December 29, 2009
115. Matoo, Amitabh, Kapil Kak and Happymon Jacob, (eds.) *India and Pakistan Pathways Ahead,* KW Publishers Pvt. Ltd. New Delhi, 2007, p. 194.
116. Drew Frederic, *The Northern Barrier of India: A Popular Account of the Jammu and Kashmir territories with illustrations* (London: Edward standard, 1877) 1st edition. Reprinted by Light and Life Publishers, Jammu, 1971.
117. Paul, R. Brass, *The Politics of India Since Independence,* 2nd edition, publisher, Cambridge University Press 1990, pp. 225-226.
118. Manjumdar, A. K and Bhanwar Singh, (eds.) *Regionalism in Indian Politics*, edited, Radha Publications, New Delhi, 1997, p. 228.
119. *Ibid;* p. 229.
120. *Ibid;* pp. 229-230.
121. Puri, Balraj, *Simmering Volcano*, op.cit, pp. 51-52.
122. Matoo, Amitabh, Kapil Kak and Happymon Jacob,(eds.), *India and Pakistan Pathways Ahead,* KW Publishers Pvt. Ltd., New Delhi, 2007, p. 196.

123. Manjumdar, A. K and Bhanwar Singh,(eds.), *Regionalism in Indian Politics*, Radha Publications, New Delhi, 1997, p. 225.
124. Behera, N. C. *Demystifying Kashmir*, Pub. Dorling Kindersley (India), Delhi, 2007, p. 117.
125. Chowdhary, Rekha and Hari Om, (eds.), *Politics of Autonomy in Jammu and Kashmir*, Vinod publishers, Jammu, p. 214.
126. The Gazette of India, New Delhi, May 9, 1995 Ministry of Law, Justice and Company Affairs, p. 1.
127. The Gazette of India, New Delhi, May 9, 1995 Ministry of Law, Justice and Company Affairs, p. 14.
128. *The Ladakh Autonomous Hill Development Council Act 1995. (LAHDC).*
129. *The Ladakh Autonomous Hill Development Council Act 1995. (LAHDC).*
130. Om, Hari and Rekha Chowdhery,(eds.), *Politics of Autonomy in Jammu and Kashmir*, Vinod publishers, Jammu, p. 214.
131. *Ibid.*
132. Prakash, Shri and Ghlum Mohammad, (eds.) *Towards understanding Kashmir Crisis,* Gyan Publishing House, New Delhi, 2002, p. 78.
133. Papathy Wig, A.R, *Faulty Planning is Ladakh's base*, Hindustan Times, April 20, 1995.
134. *Boarder Affairs Journal*, Editor Pushp Saraf, Vol. 9, No. 3, April – Junes 2008, pp. 9-10.
136. Beek Van, M. and K. B. Bertelsen (1995), *Ladakh: 'Independence' Is Not Enough* _Himal_ 8: 7-15.
137. Jina, Prem Singh, *Ladakh: Past and Present*, Gyan Publishing House, New Delhi, 2002, pp. 177-178.
138. Van Martijn, *Thoughts on the Ladakh Autonomous Hill Development council act of 1995*, Beek, Dept. of Ethnography and Social Anthropology, Aarhus University, Denmark, 1995. 135. Bray, J. (1991) *Ladakhi History and Indian Nationhood*, South Asia Research 11(2) pp. 115-133.
139. Beek, Van M. (1996), *Identity Fetishism and the Art of Representation: the Long Struggle for Regional Autonomy in Ladakh*, Unpublished Ph. D, dissertation Ithaca, NY, Cornell University.
140. Sharma, Y. R. *Political Dynamics of Jammu and Kashmir*, Anand Radhakhrishanan publisher, Jammu, pp. 187-189.
141. Spalbar, Rigzin, *Why Union Territory for Ladakh*, Epilogue Magazine, February 2010, Vol. 14, Issue 2, pp. 14-15.
142. Bose Sumantra, *The challenge in Kashmir: Democracy, Self Determination and a just Peace*, Sage Publications, New Delhi, pp. 190-191.

Chapter - 4

Regional Autonomy Models: An Analysis

Notwithstanding that decolonisation and partition of British India into the nation states of India and Pakistan have been at the root of the most entrenched political problems in the Indian sub-continent. The eruption of militancy in the state of Jammu and Kashmir, besides the other causes, is an offshoot of undemocratic and inexpedient policies of the Indian political leadership towards the state. Both the principles of democracy as well as that of political expediency were relegated to the background. Groups like Jamaat-e-Islami even decided (in the early 1970s) to contest elections so that they could articulate their demands as elected representatives.[1] Syed Ali Shah Geelani, the hard-line separatist leader, himself was elected to the State Assembly as a candidate from the Muttahida Muslim Mahaz (The Muslim United Front) in 1987. The election proved to be a turning point in the history of the Kashmiris Struggle for self-determination. The Muslim United Front was poised to win the elections by a considerable majority but this election was sabotaged by the Government of India, which feared that Muslim United Front would refuse to toe its line if it came to power.[2] The widespread rigging of this election in Jammu and Kashmir (as well as previous ones) and the indiscriminate arrests and brutal treatment of Muslim United Front workers and candidates mobilised the Kashmiris,"that peaceful methods of democracy to articulate their grievances would never work due to Indian intransigence".[3] Thus, the people of Kashmir started perceiving that a truly democratic government will never come to power in the state, for such a government reflecting the genuine aspirations of the majority of the people of Jammu and Kashmir would advocate the state's separate identity from India. Thus, it was in 1989 that some Kashmiri youth joined the existing club of those who adopted militant path with the perception to force the Indian government to allow the people of Jammu and Kashmir to determine their own political future.[4] The insurgency in Jammu and Kashmir has extracted an enormous price from the people of the state and was fuelled by the systematic erosion of democratic as well as human rights. Thus, the militancy in the State of Jammu and Kashmir can be explicated to this background of historical distrust that has secluded the relationship between the State of Jammu and Kashmir and India.[5]

After the eruption of militancy in 1989, the Indian Government promised autonomy once again. The objective behind this offer was to check the secessionist trend in Kashmir and create a favourable situation for the pro-accession parties and hold the elections. Though the situation was not favourable, yet dates for the Parliamentary elections were fixed in 1996.[6] The major regional, mainstream and proaccession party of the state, the Jammu and Kashmir National Conference, threatened to boycott these elections as its President Dr. Farooq Abdullah insisted that the quantum of autonomy should be decided before the polls. However, the Central Government remained adamant that the question of autonomy would be decided with the elected representatives of the state. Farooq Abdullah, after winning the assembly elections in 1996, concentrated on his first priority of defining, deciding and negotiating a package of autonomy for the three regions of the state.[7] For this purposes, the Jammu and Kashmir government constituted a committee, headed by Chief Minister Dr. Farooq Abdulla, on November 29, 1996, to recommend ways and means for regional autonomy to the three regions/provinces of this state. The committee submitted its twenty five page report to the state government on April 13, 1999.[8] The Regional Autonomy Committee recommended two alternate models of autonomy within Jammu and Kashmir. One was the formation of Regional/ Provincial Councils and other was the setting up of District Councils. The first model seeks to reorganise the state into eight regions/provinces to meet the requirements of devolution of power to different regions in the state.[9] The second model of the committee recommended the setting up of District Councils as an alternative to the regional/provincial councils which in coordination with Panchayat Raj institutions were supposed to work as effective agents in augmenting the processes leading to faster pace of development.[10] Though, both the models would have been proved as ideal system for meeting the aspirations of the people of either each region or each district[11] but the way the committee recommended the reconstitution of regions or provinces raised many eyebrows. The critics of both the models are of the opinion that, if not in Kashmir valley, the regional autonomy pattern as envisaged by the committee can promote communal divide in the regions of Jammu and Ladakh.[12] Their argument is that although the categorisation of the state into eight regions or provinces may not have an impact on the community character in the valley however, the said arrangement would have communal consequences in the Jammu and Ladakh regions. This is so because although the regions of the valley viz.: Kamraz, Nundabad, Maraz are Muslim dominated and therefore, do not have an impact on the communal character of the valley. However, the reconstitution of the Jammu and Ladakh regions would communally divide the regions.[13]

No doubt, the committee in its report correctly points out that (p.12) regional autonomy must not aim at satisfying ethnic urges only, but must ensure the ultimate goal of human development. However, it does not clearly explain how the division of Jammu and Kashmir into three regions and Ladakh into two is going to help to achieve the twin ends they had kept in mind. The report is silent over the basis of grouping and clubbing of the Districts (which are basically administrative units) to constitute a region.[14] Although giving additional rights and responsibilities to the new administrative units may amount to devolution of administrative authority to lower and local levels, but that is different from regional autonomy.[15] A region is not an arbitrary administrative unit but a natural one with a distinct geo-climatic, economic, or ethnocultural personality of its own. So the problems, aspirations and awareness of identity of local population have to be taken into account before regions are contributed and their boundaries are drawn.[16]

Professor K. N. Pandita, former director Centre of Central Asian Studies, University of Kashmir, argued that, "the pattern recommended by the committee is likely to sabotage the trifurcation of the state into three separate states of Kashmir, Jammu and Ladakh on religious lines. The trifurcation was being demanded by the BJP and by the Jammu Mukti Morcha. Therefore, supporting the reconstitution of the provinces, the National Conference aimed at achieving the forty five years old scheme of having 'Greater Kashmir' incorporating the three and a half Muslim-dominated districts as a separate state."[17]

Another annoyance of the report is that the committee recommended the election of each Regional Council to be held on the pattern of the State Assembly and the leader of the majority party so elected will head the council and enjoy the powers of minister of state. According to the report, under the proposed delimitation of provinces six out of eight regions would have Muslim as Council's heads because of the population character of these regions.[18] Moreover, it also didn't mention the demand of Hindu Minority in the valley as well as Punun Kashmir movement of Kashmiri Pundits. It also came without offering an alternative strategy or framework for redressing their grievances and securing their social, cultural, economic and political rights. The report also did not take notice of the Zanaskar Buddhists long standing demand for these areas to be brought under Leh's administration. Likewise, it glossed over the fact that Doda district had a significant Hindu minority alongside its Muslim majority and made no provision for safeguarding the minority's political interests.[19]

The recommendations made in the report raised some doubts because there are no monolithic political groupings of Hindus and Muslims in the Jammu region. Their political affiliations cut across ethnic, linguistic and caste lines, as well as regions. The Jammu Muslims for example, are in minority in the Jammu region but form a majority in Poonch, Rajouri and Doda districts.[20] They don't support the Bhartiya Janta Party's Hindu Politics and a separate state of Jammu, nor are they willing to be assimilated completely into the Kashmiri Muslim identity. At the same time, they don't form a separate and cohesive political group, partly because since the pre-partition leadership of Chowdhary Ghulam Abbas and Allah Rakha Sagar, no political leader has emerged to mobilise them as an independent political force in state politics.[21] Thus, any attempt to superimpose communal boundaries is not only divisive but also bound to fail for two reasons. First, these are political problems and sharpening the communal boundaries will simply not resolve them. For example, the Paharis are spread from Basoli in Kathua to Rajouri and Poonch on one side and to Uri and Keran in the Valley. Why then, does their demand for Pahari region along the line of control exclude areas in the Valley?[22] Also, if the demand is driven by the lack of economic development, one must recognise that the predominantly Hindu Hill areas south of the Chenab in Kathua, have done no better than Rajouri and Poonch.[23]

The solution lies in providing a responsive government rather than in sharpening the communal boundaries. Second, political mobilisation along the communal lines is bound to limit the social base of the political groups making these demands on the state. And without a base of mass support, they are not likely to serve their political demands.[24]

Further, it is significant to note that Regional Autonomy Committee (RAC) Report does not look autonomy as a continuum. It is rather obvious that the issue of *Regional Autonomy* is being seen as an exclusive domain of the government of Jammu and Kashmir. In other words, there is a tacit acknowledgement of the fact that diverse regions/ provinces of the Jammu and Kashmir have to negotiate their understandings and demands of *autonomy* with the centre of power located in the valley.[25] Ranbir Samaddar in his book '*The Politics of Autonomy: An Indian Experience*' accused the Regional Autonomy Committee (RAC) report of turning a blind eye to the Regional political sensibilities of Jammu and Ladakh, or for that matter Kashmir choose to deploy categories such as Provinces or Divisions.[26] The RAC came to the conclusion that, "a sharp sense of neglect and discrimination among the diverse ethnic groups of the regions of the state exists. This sense of discrimination is sharper in the regions of Jammu province particularly in the hilly and far flung areas of the province which can be substantiated from the fact that a number of memorandums have been submitted by the people from Doda, Rajouri and Poonch indicated that these groups perceive themselves belonging to different regions.[27] Thus, it has been felt that there is urgency in demarcating the regions in the state for the purpose of political and economic decentralisation of power. The history of these regions and their particular ethnic profiles supports their claims of belonging to different regions".[28] The central argument of the report, ironically, revolved around the logic of counteracting the existing understanding of the regions. It did not use the term "Region" to define the political status of Jammu or Ladakh or for that matter even Kashmir. Defining them as "Provinces" or "Divisions" for administrative convenience, the report called the earlier attempts to define these as "distinct regions" as erroneous in nature. The Report tries to redraw the "internal map" of the state of

Jammu and Kashmir without any meaningful departure from predominant, territorialised governmentality.[29]

The Regional Autonomy Committee report has also been criticised by Robert Wirsing on account of its strategic deployment of the so called "regional" territorial identities on the geopolitical chessboard by the state elite. According to Robert Wirsing, "The Regional Autonomy Report is painstakingly drafted to define the project of redrawing internal boundaries entirely in terms of 'ethnic diversity' and what it calls 'ethno–cultural-linguistic groups' ". It denies that religious identity either motivates the demand for restructuring the state's boundaries or seriously figures in the restructuring plan. The report manages somehow to discuss Kashmir's ethnography for thirty–odd pages, in fact, while only once employing the word Muslim and not even once the Hindus and Buddhists. It has been argued that, "this discourse was perceived to be "Kashmir Centric".[30] Some BJP and Congress leaders said regional autonomy be granted to the existing three regions without altering their demographic character. They said that Jammu and Kashmir is a multi-lingual, multi-religious and multi-regional state with different ethnic groups living in different parts of the area.[31] Over the centuries these ethnic and sub-ethnic groups have learnt to live in amity and once the provinces were carved out on religious or ethnic considerations it would destabilise the secular character of the state.[32] According to Balraj Puri, "the state is a having a unitary government with diverse ethnic and multi lingual character. In order to maintain the unity in diversity, the state needs a federalised type of model where the power would be decentralised to accommodate the different ethnic and linguistic groups. In this way, both unity and identity will be preserved and the tensions could be contained. By demarcating the regions on communal lines rather than secular can become a threat for the secular identity of the state".[33] However, according to Nayeem Akther, "National Conference leadership has been raising Regional Autonomy slogan but the fact is that the proposal remains a mystery not only for the people of the state but even for the government of India and National Conference itself".[34]

However, Balraj Puri had prepared another model of regional autonomy based on varied themes like Political Autonomy, Cultural Autonomy and Financial Autonomy. Though, he was the working Chairman of National Conference's Regional Autonomy Committee

Report, but later on he was dismissed from the chair.[35] Both National Conference and Balraj Puri prepared their own models according to their tastes. Puri had long since made known his opposition to any autonomy scheme that sought to redraw the map of the state along more sharply communal meaning religious lines and thus to deepen communal identities.[36] His own drafted regional autonomy model was rejected by the Government of Jammu and Kashmir in 1999 especially by the then National Conference President Dr. Farooq Abdullah which precipitated his removal as Chairman only months before scheduled submission. However, he privately published his regional autonomy report in book form soon after his departure. In this book, he called for state's administrative and political devolution in a manner that would preserve the state's unity and leave the present three regions of Jammu, Kashmir valley and Ladakh essentially intact (communally more or less heterogeneous).[37] Local autonomy was to be achieved by bolstering India's well established Panchayat Raj system. The object was to achieve decentralisation of state power and enhanced institutional representation of ethno-linguistic minorities without at the same time further entrenching the communal identities of the three regions.[38] Balraj Puri's regional autonomy model takes Panchayat Raj as a sufficient effective device for ensuring intergroup equity in Jammu and Kashmir and rejects the idea of increased convergence of the state's internal boundaries for equity among the different cultural group identities.[39]

The committee for regional autonomy in Jammu and Kashmir State under the Chairmanship of Balraj Puri aims at evolving a system to reduce regional tensions in the state not only by reconciling regional aspirations, but also its wide diversities. It seeks to provide for an equitable and balanced development of all its regions and communities, in spheres as varied as political, economic, educational, social and cultural.[40] However, in order to meet the regional aspirations, there are two choices before the people either to be assimilated and homogenised with dominant community or to seek a separate statehood. But both may not be possible or desirable in many cases. Forced uniformity not only kills creativity and healthy potentialities of regional identities but also surest way to disunity. The other alternative of separate statehood, if certain conditions are not fulfilled; like total homogeneity in separated parts, can spell disaster for these parts.[41] This leads to the inevitable third option or alternative of extending the federal principles that is what Balraj Puri has said extending the federal principle to the internal setup of the state without demarcating regions on religious basis. This will lead to the empowerment of state, district, block and the Panchayat level.[42] This whole process is called the federal continuum and it will remain incomplete if there is any link missing otherwise, it will definitely accommodate the interests and aspirations of all the ethnic identities and also protect the plural character of the state.[43] Balraj Puri's Regional autonomy model plays a very important role in making unity in diversity because it has taken care of minorities also, like schedule castes, schedule tribes and OBC's through the chain of 73rd and 74th constitutional amendment act 1992.[44] Also, the report emphasises that the heads of the district boards should not be ministers as National Conference's regional autonomy model did, but the local representatives and non-governmental organisations should be involved in the promotion of culture, language and art in the state. The proposed councils should be setup in the existing regions and the existing Ladakh Autonomous Hill Development Council act should be financially and administratively empowered.[45]

However, a vital component of regional autonomy is its economic content. Political autonomy will be more meaningful if it is accompanied by economic autonomy; which means power to raise resources, power to decide priorities and an objective and equitable formula for allocations of funds by the state to the regions.[46]

The allocation should not be based on arbitrary and subjective considerations but should take due notice of objective factors like population, area, backwardness and contribution to the state exchequer in portion to its income.[47] According to Balraj Puri, apart from the role of federalism in integrating diversities and fuller use of local resources and hence faster and equitable economic growth, there is third vital role of it i.e. power to the people and ensuring genuine democracy.[48]

Balraj Puri argues that the "federal scheme and regional autonomy approach towards Jammu and Kashmir has been also applied by other countries and they got succeeded in fulfilling their regional aspirations like, Switzerland, USA, Canada and Australia. Lately even unilingual and uni-religious countries of Europe have started transforming themselves from unitary government to a federal setups. After decentralisation experiments in France, Spain, Italy, Germany, and a small country like Belgium conceded regional autonomy to Scotland

and Wales in United Kingdom in September 1997 where predominant language and religious denomination are the same and got succeeded in mitigating their regional demands.[49] The example of Switzerland, the oldest federation of the world, is particularly striking its three ethnic units viz. Germans, French and Italians have remained united even when their mother countries went through two great world wars. Their natural sympathies with their respective countries of origin did not undermine their loyalty to Switzerland. This was entirely due to the fact that Switzerland had given maximum autonomy to its component parts and decentralised power to the maximum extent".[50]

Abdul Hamid Qazi, General Secretary Chenab Valley Hill Development Forum has welcomed the report of regional autonomy committee headed by Balraj Puri and described it as a highly balanced and representing the aspirations of the people concerned. He said, "If implemented it would prove a pivotal role in the development of neglected, far flung, backward areas of the state and over all integrated balanced development of the state which shall strengthen the unity of the people with diverse ethnic, linguistic, cultural and social characteristics".[51] According to Prof. Rekha Chowdhary, "the regions are not to be developed for their own sake. The development of the regions has to be affected for the benefit of the people residing therein. There are regions where some sections of the population have got better chances of development, living in the same region while others have continued to be deprived from the fruits of development. Therefore, the regional autonomy model prepared by Balraj Puri is a welcome step because it is expected that due attention would be paid towards the development of the ignored sections of the populace. It would remove the discrimination suffered by the people so that justice - economic, social, cultural and educational, becomes easily available to them, and the people are able to live with a full sense of security, free from fear and exploitation".[52]

However, the regional autonomy model prepared by Balraj Puri became controversial when it was found that without discussing the report with the committee members, Mr. Puri went public on it and leaked it out to the press. Another limitation of the model is its sweeping recommendations of having a five tier system of governance ranging from State to Panchayats. Its implementation would have, in the ultimate analysis, left the state government with no powers.[53] Further, as some members claimed that certain memoranda that had come from places like Doda district were not taken into account by Balraj Puri. Secondly, some doubts were raised as for as the devolution of power under the scheme of 73rd and 74th constitutional amendment acts when the Panchayat Raj Act of 1989 has not so far been amended. Finally, how would a governmental institutions like academy of art, culture and languages ensure people's initiatives in promotion of the plural cultural traditions.[54]

According to Ashutosh Kumar, "regional autonomy model despite gives some suggestions to remove the regional imbalances and fulfill the regional grievances and differences, it raised many questions like what are the subjects that should be delegated to the regions, what should be the basis of allocation of funds between and within the region and what should be the institutions to deal with the subjects delegated to the regions?[55] What steps should be taken for the promotion of language, literature and culture of various linguistic and ethnic groups and what positive measures apart from constitutional provisions including political, cultural, social should be adopted to promote emotional harmony and unity of the state and remove all causes of tensions between ethnic and religious community and what special measures are needed to identify and protect interests of the various groups and community".[56] All these recommendations were not implemented but the committee under the chairmanship of Balraj Puri was constituted only in response to the compelling political circumstances prevailing in the regions of Jammu and Ladakh.[57]

Moreover, with the passage of time, another model of regional autonomy and a framework for the resolution of Kashmir dispute was prepared by the Jammu and Kashmir People's Democratic Party. But this model was very much different from the other two models in the sense; it has attempted to unite the two alienated parts of the whole Jammu and Kashmir (Pak Occupied Kashmir and Indian Occupied Kashmir). While as the other two models have focused only on the integration of different regions within Indian occupied Kashmir only. In an interview with Nayeem Ahmad spokesperson of Peoples Democratic Party, he said, "the party framed in the self-rule document as an internally consistent framework and indicative direction for Kashmir resolution. It has tried to contextualise the issue at various levels and drawn the contours of a process for building sustainable peace in the state and the region. The basic premises and sum and substance of the Self Rule document lie in trying to suggest a creative framework for resolution of the issue without compromising the sovereignty of the two nation states involved".[58] The Self Rule document reads and moves forward various proposals and measures, to address both the internal and external dimensions of the problem in a manner that it would be realistic and practical i.e. for the ideals of justice and empowerment for all the people of the state. The Self Rule document has also made an effort for fulfilling the aspirations of all the three regions and sub-regions of the state.[59] It can also end the long mental siege of the people by making whole Jammu and Kashmir a demilitarised free economic zone and an experimental ground for South Asian Association of Regional Cooperation. According to Zulfikar Abbasi, President of Muzaffarabad Chamber of Commerce,"The initiation of free economic zone will become the foundation for strong intra-Kashmir trade. The opening of the cross- LOC trade is the revival of 60 year old ties that had been snapped due to hostilities between India and Pakistan.[60] This is going to be one of the biggest confidence building measures and all hurdles will be removed with increase in frequency and volume of the trade. It will also lay the foundation for peace ties for future generations. However, the big challenge is how to turn this opportunity into sustainable and profitable venture.[61] It should not be overlooked that there is a strong anti-trade lobby that do not care if Indian and Pakistani traders do business and make profits but try to disrupt the forward movement on the basis of their flawed ideological notions over Kashmir".[62]

Broadly speaking, the self-rule document seems to be focused on the reformatting of the state's constitutional relationship with the Centre. Precisely, the document seeks retroaction to restore state's authority and to that extent curtail Centre's jurisdiction. The People's Democratic Party patron Mufti Mohammad Sayeed said that his party wants President of India should not have powers to dissolve Jammu and Kashmir Assembly as enshrined in Article 356. He says, "I think to resolve the Kashmir issue we can't assume a fixed state. Self-Rule, besides other constitutional guarantees, talks about the elected Governor, demilitarisation and respects regional and sub-regional aspirations". He further said, "The self-Rule document would politically empower the people of Kashmir by seeking to undo acts of constitutional subversion that the state has suffered over since accession. We seek full control of the people of this state over their identities, political preferences and administrative arrangements". Self-Rule includes the revival of the elected Sadre-e-Riyasat and scrapping of laws repugnant to Kashmir's political aspirations. The authority of the state legislature should be revived and it should have full powers to amend the state constitution.[63] The Self Rule document also provides a workable and structural format for cross line of control (LOC) relations in the state. Self-Rule as a political philosophy is being articulated around the conception of federalism and confederation that allows for sharing power between two levels of government, for the sharing of sovereignty in a coordinated but not subordinated to one another; each exercising supreme sovereignty in its constitutional prerogatives.[64] The comprehensive formulation of Self Rule has three components. First consists of the new political superstructure that integrates the regions and empowers the sub-regions.

Second a phased economic integration that transcends boarders and last but not the least is constitutional restructuring that ensures sharing of sovereignty without compromising the political sovereignty of either nation.[65] Essentially, the document is best examined from two main angles: the internal (autonomy) angle and the external (cross–LOC interaction) angle. Much as the document seeks to repudiate, its content bears fairly close resemblance to the 'autonomy' plan of the National Conference. To analyze the Self Rule document enunciated by Peoples Democratic Party (PDP) also needs to be evaluated in relation to the party's position on the political grid – map. The dividing line of the politics in this state is 'accession' one is either for, or against the accession. That is the crux of the problem and also the basic issue of the dispute.[66] The separatists see it in no other way. On the other hand, Peoples Democratic Party, like National Conference and other mainstream groups, is on what might call the 'right' side of the accession. That position determines the variation in the interpretation of the 'dispute' and projection of its 'resolution'. In political terms, the Peoples Democratic Party's interpretation of the 'dispute for which the party's Self Rule document goes on to prescribe a 'solution' are not the same as that of the separatists.[67] While, the thrust of the National Conference's autonomy plan is on restoration of pre–1953 status of the center–state constitutional format, the self-rule idea goes further up to 1947and more importantly, lends a wider (external dimension) to the concept in the context of the recent developments like re-opening of Srinagar-Muzaffarabad road.68 The Peoples Democratic Party's document proposes a legislative superstructure comprising elected representatives from both sides of the line of control. It also advocates qualified 'shared sovereignty' short of touching the existing 'territorial sovereignty' of India and Pakistan over Jammu and Kashmir.[69] Resolution of Kashmir dispute lies in the unification of both parts of the state divided by the LOC which would be possible only when there would be no borders between people of two parts of Kashmir. While the Self Rule formula suggests making the borders irrelevant.[70]

The Peoples Democratic Party's (PDP's) document painstakingly enumerates the long list of differences between its Self Rule plan and the National Conference's Autonomy plan. It points out that the basic difference is between 'framework and empowerment'. Para 63 of the Self Rule document says, the problem in Jammu and Kashmir has been that while it has been fairly autonomous, it has been ineffective to bring about the results it desires. The problem with the pure autonomist view point is that it confuses autonomy with empowerment.[71] However, like autonomy plan, the self-rule document seeks revocation of the post–1953 federal laws and constitutional provisions applied to Jammu and Kashmir. It also seeks restoration of the institutions of (elected) Sadri–Riyasat and Prime Minister for Jammu and Kashmir.[72]

According to Mohammad Sayed Malik, "historical experience does not uphold the faith invested by Peoples Democratic Party in its remedial prescription. To cite just one instance, the worst assault on the state's autonomous character occurred in 1953 both the 'framework' and 'empowerment' were very much in place. Jammu and Kashmir was theoretically semi–independent then. The center's jurisdiction was limited to only defense, foreign affairs and communication as specified in the Maharaja's instrument of accession.[73] The Delhi Agreement of 1952 was yet to be implemented when Sheikh Abdulla was arbitrarily dismissed from power in August 1953 which was the starting point of an unstoppable slide in Jammu and Kashmir's state's autonomy in every sense of the term.[74] Constitutional safeguards sought by the self-rule document have thus been already robbed the credibility in the light of what happened in 1953. Falling back upon the worn out plank is less convincing. Popular support for accession in 1947 was eroded by what happened in 1953 and what all followed. Mere restoration of that vulnerable position at this point of time is not going to wash".[75]

Self-Rule Document argues that Article 370 had been rendered a 'permanent' feature of the federal constitution by the manner and mechanism of its operationalisation and its consequent linkage with the accession. The document holds that the two had become 'inter-dependent', meaning that Article 370 goes the accession created by federal legislature. The constitution itself describes it as a'temporary' provision which naturally and tacitly means that it is not permanent and thereby, can be erased at any time, obviously by parliament. Practical wisdom rules out the possibility of Indian parliament ever agreeing to the interpretation that Article 370 and accession of Jammu and Kashmir are interdependent.[76] The PDP's stand is that the solution would 'evolve' out of the road map (Self Rule Document). That again is not acceptable to the separatists. So the dispute refuses to go away. Compulsions of local politics have made the Kashmir's mainstream class to practice the fine art of stretching the term 'alienation' to seek dilution of the 'accession' via autonomy plan or the self-rule idea without saying so. That circumvention evokes the accusation of 'blasphemy' (against accession) from across the Jawaher Tunnel.[77]

M. G. Hassan writes in Kashmir Times, "another deficiency in the document is that the edifice it seeks to raise rests largely upon the quick sands of Indo-Pak good will whose course is dependent upon numerous variables. Any upset in the fragile peace process or bilateral dialogue is bound to reflect upon the prospects of the proposition set out in the document. Even otherwise also, going by the miserly implementation of the mutually agreed Confidence Building Measures like bus and trade services across the line of control, hoping for dream-like magnanimity from both the sides is like asking for the moon.[78] The self-rule document is therefore useless as any other document made earlier or to be made in future unless equal to or greater than plebiscite or self-determination or at least what victims (Kashmiris including others) demand from the encroacher (India) as well as from grabber (Pakistan). The people of Kashmir directly and others indirectly are demanding the right of self-determination or Plebiscite as the case may be and anything less than that is simply dilution or there is no fun to waste time and energy on making these stupid documents. It is better to have status quo than these insufficient Kashmir resolution road maps like autonomy and self-rule documents. These Kashmiri crooks will create more trouble for the masses".[79]

Sayed Malik says that, "according to Mufti's Self Rule theory, Self (means himself or herself from PDP never your good self) must be self-less residing (on rotation basis) in Jammu and Kashmir and Rule must have youth fullness and faithfulness in ruthlessness coming indirectly or directly from Metro Delhi, whether by air, tunnel or road. He also says, the document is a mixture of many things mostly adopted from Sajjad Lone's vision document "Achievable Nationhood" particularly the joint management system, joint economic system etc. and the rotational position of the Head of the state mentioned in the Self Rule document has been originally wrote by M.G. Hassan Mukhtar in Srinagar based Urdu Weekly "Chattan" on 14th April, 2008 against the policy of Mufti Mohammad Sayeed and G.N. Azad Coalition Government that these two leaders have almost induced a concept of regional favouritism".[80] Therefore, it seems that both the National Conference's autonomy resolution and PDP's Self Rule document fall miserably short of providing credible safeguards for protecting the individual freedom and liberty. What use is the autonomy of full or greater variety or self-rule when the system is left free to trample the basic freedom with impunity? Because past as well as present experience is proof of the lethal lacuna in overlooking this vital consideration while floating ideas for redeeming the situation.[81]

Though the People's Democratic Party's self-rule doctrine is generally being considered as a bold plan conceived by a major mainstream political party in Kashmir, some political players beg to differ. Political parties in the state have questioned the timing of the PDP's proposal that advocates "shared sovereignty" of an integrated and united Jammu and Kashmir between India and Pakistan. Representatives of the mainstream parties are of the view that proposal has been made public to gain political mileage.[82] According to Abdul Gani Vakil, "The purpose of unveiling the proposal at the election time is to seek votes. This is a borrowed concept of General Pervez Musharraf, only aimed at exploiting voters. When Mufti Sahib was the Chief Minister, he didn't talk about Self Rule or Dual Currency. Any proposal would be acceptable only when it is accepted by all parties, including Hurriyat Conference".[83] According to Omar Abdullah, "the fact that Peoples Democratic Party (PDP) chooses this particular time to release their Self-rule document shows their non-seriousness. They were in the government for last six years. They could have brought it to the assembly, put it in the form of a resolution so that there was a discussion on it. Then this document could have been discussed during the round tables or workers group meetings".[84] According to Hakim Yasin, "I do not see any difference between PDP's self-rule proposal and the National Conference's Autonomy Report. There is nothing new in this (Self-rule) report. I don't understand why they shy away from calling it the autonomy proposal. In fact, the Peoples Democratic Party (PDP) has taken some of the ideas discussed during the meetings of working Group on Centre-State relations and incorporated them in the report".[85]

Sardar Sikendar Hayat Khan, Prime Minister of Azad Kashmir, had also proposed the formula of dividing the whole Jammu and Kashmir on the basis of religion known as "the Chenab divide of Kashmir" in 1960's.[86] It practically means the division of the culturally, geographically, historically and economically distinct Jammu and Ladakh regions along religious lines and the merger of all the Muslim-majority areas—Doda, Poonch, Rajouri and Kargil—of these two regions. It also means the segregation of certain Hindu-majority areas in the Jammu region and their merger with a predominantly Muslim Kashmir.[87] However, the implementation of the Chenab formula would also result in a vertical division of the Doda district's tehsils of Kishtwar, Ramban, Thathri and Banihal which are inhabited by people of both faiths. The result would be the segregation of the Gujjar and Bakerwal Muslim-dominated areas of Mahore and Gool Gulabgarh from the Hindu-majority Udhampur district and their integration with Kashmir which is located beyond the Pir Panjal, the mountain range that divides Jammu from the Valley. Similarly, the Buddhist-dominated Zanskar area would also become part of 'Greater Kashmir', because it is located within the Shia-majority Kargil. The only Muslim-majority areas which would remain unaffected by the Chenab formula would be Gandoh, Bhalessa and Bunjwah of Doda district, since they fall on the wrong side of the river Chenab.[88] It needs to be underlined that the people of these areas are vehemently opposed to the Chenab formula. They believe that its implementation would seal their political and economic fate and endanger their religious and social life. In fact, the Chenab formula if implemented could lead to a communal holocaust. It would go counter to everything that secular and pluralistic nations like India values.[89]

According to the 'Chenab Formula', Pakistan may consider 'Doaba', a narrow strip of land between Chenab and Ravi rivers in the suburbs of Shakargarh (distt. Sialkot) stretching up to Chamb, Dhodha and Rajwari districts as international border, even the town of Kargil might go to India under this 'give and take' but from Kargil upward, India will have to agree to give territory to Pakistan. Most of the districts in Jammu and on the left bank of the Chenab are Hindu majority in the state of Jammu and Kashmir while in most of the districts on the west side of the Chenab, the Muslims are predominant.[90] However, Pakistan may agree to forego its claim over Buddhist majority Ladakh region as well, but there will be no compromise on the Valley. The Muslim majority Valley is the main area of concern for Pakistan as Islamabad wants control over it. The Valley in Chenab formula will be partially autonomous but there will be major changes on the borderline to adjust tehsils and towns surrounding the Valley between India and Pakistan.[91] Inspite of this, the solution would require the voluntary agreement of India to give up territory which it wants to retain. It is impossible to see what benefit India could derive from the transfer of so much land, and why the government or the inhabitants of the region who are not contesting their status would ever agree to such a solution.[92]

However, most of the supporters believe that Chenab Formula could easily solve Kashmir Issue where Hindu, Buddhist Majority Regions of Jammu and Ladakh go to India (Left Bank of Chenab) and Kashmir valley goes to Pakistan (Mostly Right Bank of Chenab). But doing so will dissolve the Indus Water Treaty and Pakistan would then have only complete control over only the Indus, Jhelum and some of their tributaries.[93] Also, in response to BJP's support to Chenab Formula, the former Chief Minister, Farooq Abdullah opposed the suggestion by disclosing that a formula has been prepared to divide the state. Speaking in the State Assembly he said, "That new borders are being created in Jammu and Ladakh along the River Chenab and Malbek. National Conference will not divide the state but a formula is under review to divide Kashmir in New Delhi. Under this formula, there will be new international border along with Chenab, Leh and Kargil. It is a pity that these people who opposed the division of Kashmir have now finalised the proposed formula for Kashmir division. It has been planned to divide Kashmir in four parts. While criticising Bhartiya Janta Party and Congress, he said that these parties have no courage to wage war. Kashmiris are being subjected to oppression for the last fifty years. Lashing out at Bhartiya Janta Party, he said that in fact, this party is responsible for Kashmir situation".[94] According to Schaffer, "United States is actively working on the formula to divide Kashmir and the ruling party of India Bhartiya Janta Party has also agreed to it. He further says that the Kashmir division formula has been presented by study group in United States which has the complete support of United States (US). This formula has been named Chenab Formula under which an independent state comprising the Muslim-dominated areas has been proposed".[95] Sikander's ideas were strongly criticised by opposition leaders in Muzaffarabad. Leaders of the hard-line religious party Jamaat-e-Islami, have declared that nothing short of a plebiscite is acceptable to them. Opposition has also come from leaders of the main Kashmiri political groups in Indian-administered Kashmir, the All-Party Hurriyat Conference (though some of their main leaders were individually supporting the idea) and even the Awami National Party in Pakistan has also rejected the Chenab formula on religious grounds.[96]

The study has also attempted to analyse the Ladakh Autonomous Hill Development Council (LAHDC) with its broad perspectives and its feasibility vis-à-vis addressing the regional problems within Jammu and Kashmir state. On 9th May, 1995, Ladakh after a long struggle of peaceful agitation, protests, hartals and sacrifices got included into the Gazette of India as Ladakh Autonomous Hill Development Council Act (LAHDC).[97] The Act provided an Autonomous Hill Council for Leh and Kargil and inter-district advisory Councils with tenure of five years. Each Council would have twenty six territorial constituencies. The sitting MLA's and MP's would be ex–officio members, four nominated by the state government. The nominees include one Muslim, one woman and two eminent persons. The Council constitutes a cabinet of five members with one Muslim. The executive powers of the council included allotment, use and occupation of land vested in the council by the government, formulation of annual plan and development programme, budget (plan and non-plan), special measures for employment generation and poverty alleviation, promotion of cooperative institutions and local culture and languages.[98] The council was further empowered to levy taxes and collect state taxes on behalf of the government. The inter-district council has to advise the district council on matters of common interest to both districts, resolving their differences and preservation of communal harmony in Ladakh.[99]

However, it appears as if there will be freedom from the clutches of political and economic centralisation invariably both at the levels of state as well as Centre, and there will be genuine devolution of powers and developmental activities. Although, it also assumed opening of new vistas for the people of the area and will bring unity among the people of Ladakh where all political groups irrespective of religion, ideology and political affiliation had rallied around to demand an Autonomous Hill Council.[100] As per the past experience the council has not been able to do much for the people of the area and the state of affairs remains the same. Due to the deficiency of funds, the council is severely constrained in its attempt to give any shape to development projects.[101]

After a decade of operation, the Hill Council has failed adequately to address the local issues. Many elected councillors have found that "their de-facto powers are limited by the state governments attempt to sabotage their work." Soon after the first Ladakh Hill Council started functioning, the National Conference government led by Farooq Abdullah–who had bitterly opposed the council concept–had come to power.[102] It resorted to stonewalling tactics in approving the budget or releasing funds that, in view of the short working season in Ladakh, often made it impossible to implement local projects. All major projects, especially those for generating hydroelectric power, still had to be cleared by the state government which often did not come through.[103] As it is mentioned in the Ladakh Autonomous Hill Council Act 1995 that the government shall provide funds under the Plan and non-Plan budget to the council to be credited to the council fund as per budgetary requirements as approved by the government. The funds shall be released as per the normal budget.[104] Moreover, the Hill Council was merely another addition to an already crowded field of political–administrative bodies characterised by fragmented and overlapping competences among agencies whose agendas and interests vary profoundly. The Chief Executive Councillor, who runs the council on day-to-day basis, often clashes with those higher on the administrative ladder.[105]

The pronouncement of power decentralisation by the state government with the move to hold Panchayat elections further haunts the Ladakh Autonomous Hill Development Council (LAHDC) leadership with a fear of overlapping of powers of the council's relevance. Possibility of confusion between the Councillors and the elected Panchayat members from any one halqua regarding their functional position may also generate a feud between the two bodies. In any case, it will be the common masses that will be the ultimate sufferers.[106] Therefore, talking at the functional level the observation is complete failure and meaningless, because administrative powers are dispersed among the Hill Council and other governmental agencies, such as the Desert Development Agency which commands a vast area classified as "waste land". and plans development activities related to water management and land conservation.[107] The interests of an Autonomous Council always comes in conflict with the earlier package of democracy at the grass-root level i.e. Panchayat Raj System. The two cannot and should not co-exist and it may lead to a conflict situation if the Panchayat system in such cases is taken to its logical cohesion. Because of all these deficiencies the council led to the revival of the demand for Union Territory Status for Ladakh.[108]

Moreover, the introduction of Hill Council for Ladakh has raised hue and cry throughout Jammu and Kashmir. Pahari leaders have proposed the creation of a new Pahari region, separating predominantly Muslim Rajouri–Poonch from Jammu division with a separate Autonomous Hill Council with Leh pattern and same is the case with Kargil within Ladakh which also demanded Autonomous Council.[109] Later on, in 2002 the Jammu and Kashmir Coalition Government led by Mufti Sayeed granted similar autonomy to Kargil also. Thus, the division of Ladakh in two parts and absence of a common regional authority the people of the two communities in Leh and Kargil started drifting in divergent directions.[110] Another demand for an Autonomous Hill Council has come from the Chenab valley region for their regional grievances which consists of Doda, Gool–Gulabgradh Tehsil, Gasantgarh of Udhampur district and Lohai Malhar and Bani of Kathua District, along with a schedule tribe status. The demand for devolution of power at the sub-regional level exists parallel to the demand for regional autonomy is raised from the urban centres of the region while the demand for Hill Council or the sub-regional autonomy is raised from the backward areas of the region.[111] In the workshop organised by Jammu University on intra- Jammu and Kashmir, there were many analysts who questioned the success of the Ladakh Autonomous Hill Development Council (LAHDC) model of political devolution. There was a feeling that it had simply failed because of being too much top-down, and there were many other layers of governance like the Panchayat system that had come into collision with its governance. Seeing from another angle, the model gave the Ladakh Autonomous Hill Development Council (LAHDC) the entire say in the use of financial allocations made to the region.[112] The devolution of powers have helped Ladakh to frame an educational curriculum which the region sees best for itself. It helped the region to have local news which protects its local economy and environment. It helped it in keeping economic and other outside interests under check which may have the potential of changing the region's demography, religious value system, culture and environment.[113] According to Nawang Rigzin, "Ladakh Autonomous Hill Council which has led Ladakh fast changing for the betterment its people are awaking for emancipation. The non-governmental sector is getting very active. Local organisations are playing a leading role in protection and preservation of culture and environment. Though there are certain bureaucratic hurdles in the way but NGO's are playing a remarkable role. Education is getting top priority. In 1975, only five Ladakhis were studying in Delhi University but today at least five hundred students are studying in Delhi and Jawaharlal Nehru University that is the changing face of Ladakh because of introduction of LAHDC here".[114] He further said, "Ladakh is today accessible than it has been since, arguably, the period of 1850's when the "Greater Game" came into play, resulting in a degree of hardening of boundaries between Central and South Asia and between Tibet and South Asia (Prior to this Ladakh, of course was on the highway of trade). Isolation seems no more, resulting in receiving the benefits of "mainstream" awareness of it. Second, the communications and transport revolutions have resulted in unprecedented awareness among the people of Ladakh about the events around the world. So its strategic location and tourism also have resulted in substantial economic prosperity for its inhabitants".[115] According to Sidiq Wahid, "The granting of the Ladakh Autonomous Hill Development Council Act to Leh and subsequently to Kargil district has been welcomed, largely due to the good use it has been put by Ladakhis towards development and social welfare. And in fact the Ladakh experience should be used as a model for the rest of the state, whilst guarding against fragmentation".[116]

Notes

1. Praveen Swami, *India, Pakistan and the secret jihad, the covert war in Kashmir, 1947-2004*, Routledge Taylor and Francis group, New York, 2007, pp. 158-159.
2. Malik, Iffat, *Kashmir Ethnic Conflict, International Dispute*, Oxford University Press, 2005, pp.159-160.
3. Bose, Sumantra, *Roots of conflict and paths to peace,* Vistor Publications, New Delhi, 2003, pp.185-186.
4. Paul, T. V. (ed.), *The India-Pakistan conflict an Enduring Rivalry,* Cambridge University Press, 2005, pp. 213-214.
5. Wirsing Robert, G., *India, Pakistan and the Kashmir Dispute on Regional conflicts and its Resolution*, St. Martins Press, New York, 1994, p. 113.
6. Kaur, Ravinderjit, *Why Autonomy to Kashmir*, Institute of Peace and Conflict Studies, September 2003.
7. HabibullahWajahut, *My Kashmir conflict and the prospects of enduring peace*, United States Institute of Peace, 2008, pp. 102-103.
8. *Regional Autonomy Committee Report* Govt. of Jammu and Kashmir, 1999, p. 2.
9. Kashmir Times, Dated April 17, 1999.
10. *Ibid.*
11. Aseer Kishtwari, *Focus on Jammu and Kashmir*, Crescent Publications, Jammu, 2006, p. 556.
12. Greater Kashmir, Dated July 8, 2000.
13. According to the Committee, the segmentation/ reconstitution of the Kashmir province is: *the Kamaraz region* consisting of districts of Baramulla and Kupwara, *the Nundabad region* consisting of Budgam and Srinagar Districts, *the Maraz* province comprise of Anantnag and Pulwama districts. The suggested the reconstitution of the Jammu region into three provinces- *the Chenab valley* comprising of the districts of Doda and Mahore Tehsile of Udhampur district, *the Jammu province* comprising of the districts of Jammu, Kathua and Udhampur, excluding Mahore Tehsile and *Pirpanchal* consisting of Poonch and Rajouri Districts. *Leh and Kargil districts* would be two separate provinces. However, the reconstitution of provinces or regions recommended for the Jammu division would promote communal divide because in Hindu-dominated areas of Jammu, Kathua and Udhampur have been included in Jammu province. The Muslim dominated Mahore Tehsile

has been delinked from Udhampur district and included in the Muslim dominated Doda area under proposed Chenab valley. Similarly, two Muslim dominated belts of Poonch and Rajouri have been grouped under the proposed Pirpanchal province. So far as Ladakh is concerned, the committee recommended two separate provinces Kargil and Leh would further enhance communal polarisation between the Shia-dominated Kargil and Buddhist-dominated Leh district.

14. *Regional Autonomy Committee report,* Govt. of Jammu and Kashmir, 1999, p. 12.
15. Kashmir Times, April 27, 1999.
16. Greater Kashmir, August 25, 2000.
17. Kashmir Times, April 25, 1999.
18. Greater Kashmir, July 8, 2000.
19. Behera, N. C. *Demystifying Kashmir*, Dorling Kindersley Publisher (India), Delhi, 2007, p.135.
20. Greater Kashmir, 25 August, 2000.
21. Behera, N. C. *Demystifying Kashmir*, Dorling Kindersley Publisher (India), Delhi, 2007, p. 138.
22. Nayar, V. K. *Crossing the Frontiers of Conflict*, Shipra Publisher, New Delhi, 2005, p. 207.
23. Greater Kashmir, August 25, 2000.
24. Kashmir Times, April 27, 1999.
25. Ganguly, Sumit, *The Kashmir Question Retrospect and Prospect*, Frank CASS, Great Britain, 2003, p. 22.
26. Samaddar, Ranabir, (ed.), *The Politics of Autonomy – Indian Experience*, Sage Publication, New Delhi, 2005, p. 151.
27. Ganguly, Sumit, *The Kashmir Question Retrospect and Prospect*, Frank CASS, Great Britan, 2003, p. 22.
28. *Regional Autonomy Committee report Government of Jammu and Kashmir*, 1999, p. 8.
29. *Ibid;* p. 9.
30. Robert, G. Wirsing, *Kashmir in the shadows of war, Regional Rivalries in a Nuclear Age*, Pub. M.E. Sharpe, New York, 2002, p. 203.
31. Greater Kashmir, September 21, 2000.
32. Wirsing Robert, G. *Kashmir in the shadows of war, Regional Rivalries in a Nuclear Age*, Pub. M.E. Sharpe, New York, 2002, p. 205.
33. *Interview with Balraj Puri,* Dated 14th February 2011.
34. *Interview with Nayeem Akther,* Dated 12th February 2011.
35. Habibullah Wajahut, *My Kashmir conflict and the prospects of enduring peace,* United States Institute of Peace, 2008, p. 103.

36. Puri, Balraj, *Regional Autonomy Committee Report*, Jay Kay Book House, Jammu, p. 47.
37. *Economic and Political Weekly,* April 1999.
38. Puri, Balraj, *Jammu on the Brink*, the Hindu, August 21, 2001.
39. Balraj Puri, *Basis for a Dialogue on Kashmir* in Manzoor Fazili (ed.) *Kashmir Predilection*, Gulshan Pub., Srinagar, 1988, pp. 133-134.
40. Chowdhary, Reeta Tremblay, *Regional Autonomy versus Integration*, Kashmir Times, April 20, 1999.
41. Greater Kashmir, July 8, 2000.
42. *Economic and Political Weekly,* August 23, 2008.
43. Puri, Balraj, *Regional Autonomy Report (J&K) in 1999*, Jay Kay Publishers, Jammu, pp. 3-4.
44. *Interview with Rekha Chowdhary,* Dated 16 February 2011.
45. Jain, L. C. (ed.), *Decentralisation and local governance*, Pub. Orient Longman, New Delhi, 2005, pp. 97-98.
46. *Human Rights journal*, issue July – August, 2002, pp. 4.
47. *Interview with Balraj Puri,* Dated 14th February 2011.
48. Puri, Balraj, *Regional Autonomy Committee Report (J&K) in 1999*, Jay Kay Publishers, Jammu, p. 5.
49. Prof. Rehmatullah, *Regional Autonomy Experiments in other countries* in Puri Balraj, *Regional Autonomy Report (J&K) in 1999*, Jay Kay Publishers, Jammu, pp. 73-74.
50. *Interview with Balraj Puri,* Dated 14th February 2011.
51. Kashmir Times, April 21, 1999.
52. *Interview with Prof. Rekha Chowdhary,* Dated 16 February 2011.
53. Greater Kashmir, July 8, 2000.
54. Kumar, Ashutosh, *Some thoughts on the debate on Autonomy in Jammu and Kashmir*, Mainstream, December 23, 2000, p. 74.
55. Greater Kashmir, July 8, 2000.
56. Mandala, Sunita, *Politics of State Autonomy and Regional Identity*, Kalpaz Publications, Delhi, 2006, p. 194.
57. Kashmir Times, Wednesday, April 21, 1999.
58. *Interview with Nayeem Akther,* Dated 12th February 2011.
59. *Election Manifesto in 2008*, Jammu and Kashmir Peoples Democratic Party.
60. Daily Excelsior, October 9, 2008.
61. Greater Kashmir, October 19, 2008.
62. Daily Excelsior, October 9, 2008.
63. Sayeed Bashrat, *Mufti Finally Unveils PDP's Self Rule,* Kashmir Times, October 26, 2008.

64. Greater Kashmir, November 2, 2008.
65. The Tribune, November 25, 2008. Chandigarh, India.
66. Kashmir Times, October 20, 2008.
67. Shujjat Bukhari, *PDP Unveils Self Rule Frame Work for Kashmir*, The Hindu, October 26, 2008.
68. Greater Kashmir, October 28, 2008.
69. Mohammad Sayeed Malik, *More than autonomy but less than a viable roadmap,* Kashmir Times, November 19, 2008.
70. Greater Kashmir, October 19, 2008.
71. Greater Kashmir, October 26, 2008.
72. Perveez Majeed, *who is an Indian agent, Pro India Kashmiri Parties at logger heads*, Srinagar 8th February 2007.hptt///. Kashmiraffairs.org.in.
73. Greater Kashmir, November, 2, 2008.
74. Sagar Daya Sharma, *PDP has intelligent game plan; appears training the decade's old NC roadmap,* American Chronicle, Kashmir Affairs, September 8, 2009.
75. Mohammad Sayeed Malik, *More than autonomy but less than a viable roadmap*, Kashmir Times, November 19, 2008.
76. Sagar Daya, *Greater Autonomy or Self Rule*; *What difference does it make*, Kashmir Times, November 7, 2009.
77. Sagar Daya Sharma, *PDP has intelligent game plan; appears training the decade's old NC roadmap*, American Chronicle, Kashmir Affairs, September 8, 2009.
78. M.G. Hassan Mukhtar, *Befooling people is called Self Rule*, Kashmir Times, October 27, 2008.
79. Kashmir Times, October 27, 2008.
80. Kashmir Times, October 4, 2008.
81. Kashmir Times, October 28, 2008.
82. Himalayan Mail, October 27, 2008.
83. *Interview with Ab. Gani Vakil,* Dated 17th February 2011.
84. Himalayan Mail, October 27, 2008.
85. *Interview with Nayeem Akther,* Dated 18th February 2011.
86. Peter Iyon, *Conflict between India and Pakistan; An Encyclopedia*", ABC – CLIO, 2008, p. 161.
87. Khaled Ahmad, *Second Opinion; what is the Chenab Formula*, Daily Times, July, 2003.
88. Greater Kashmir, June 21, 2000.
89. Tikekar Maneesha, *Across the Wagah; an Indian's Sojourn in Pakistan*, Biliophite South Asia, 2004, p. 120.

90. Khaled Ahmed, *Second opinion: What is the Chenab Formula?* The Daily Times, 3 July 2003.
91. Wirsing Robert, *Kashmir in the shadows of war*, M.E. Sharpe, 2003, p. 25.
92. Malik Hafeez, *U.S relations with Afghanistan and Pakistan, the* imperial Oxford University Press, 2008, p. 114.
93. http://www.strategicforesight.com/finalsettlement/chp9options.pdf.
94. Greater Kashmir, June 21, 2000.
95. Haward B. Schaffer, *The limits of influence; America's role in Kashmir*, Brookings Institute Press, 2009, p. 88.
96. Amjad Mahmood, *ANP rejects Chenab formula*, The Dawn, June 10, 2003.
97. *The Gazette of India,* New Delhi, May 9, 1995 Ministry of Law, Justice and Company Affairs, p.1.
98. Greater Kashmir, July 1, 2000.
99. *TheLadakh Autonomous Hill Development Council Act. 1995*.
100. Arjimand Hussain Talib, *A Collective Suffering*, Greater Kashmir, December 13, 2009.
101. Om, Hari, *Politics of Autonomy in Jammu and Kashmir*, Vinod Publisher Jammu 1999, p. 215.
102. P. Kumar, *Kashmir Return to Democracy*, Cosmo Publications India, 1996, pp. 64-66.
103. Beek Martijn Van, *Making a difference; Reflections on Decentralisation, Recognition and Empowerment,* Polson Institute of Global Studies, Cornell University Press, September 21, 2001, p.12.
104. Kumar, P. *Kashmir Return to Democracy*, Cosmo Publications India, 1996, pp. 64-66.
105. Chattopadhyay, *Ethnic Composition and Crisis in South Asia*, Global Vision Pub., Delhi, 2003, p. 216.
106. Behera, N. C. *Demystifying Kashmir*, Pub Dorling Kindersley (India) Delhi 2007, p. 119.
107. Kumar, P. *Kashmir Return to Democracy*, Cosmo Publications India, 1996, pp. 64-66.
108. Martijn Van Beek, *Making a difference; Reflections on Decentralisation, Recognition and Empowerment,* Polson Institute of Global Studies, Cornell University Press, September 21, 2001, p.13.
109. Om, Hari, *Politics of Autonomy in Jammu and Kashmir*, Vinod Publisher Jammu, 1999, p. 215.
110. Kaul, *Kashmir Crisis*, Suman Publications, Srinagar 1991, pp. 71-72.
111. Rekha Chowdhary, *The politics of regional identity,* epilogue Magazine, October 2009, pp. 18-19.

112. Arjimand Hussain Talib, *A Collective Suffering*, Greater Kashmir, December 13, 2009.

113. *Ibid.*

114. *Ladakh is a unique cultural, geographical and ethnic identity*, Interview with Nawang Rigzin Jora by Zaffar Chowdhary, November 2007, pp. 16-17.

115. *Ibid.*

116. *Ladakh experience should be used as a model for the rest of the state*, interview with Prof. Siddiq Wahid February 2011, pp. 18-19.

Chapter - 5

Summary and Conclusion

Jammu and Kashmir is a heterogeneous state with varied geographical regions and sub-regions, representing different climates, flora and fauna. People possess different ethnic backgrounds, profess different faiths, follow different cultural traditions and speak different languages. What is more significant is that people living in these regions are yet to attain a uniform level of development. The internal politics of the state, marked by inter-regional tensions, has influenced the attitude of the people on the question of their external affiliations. In each of the three regions of the state, a different attitude to the question of accession can be clearly noticed from the very day of the state's accession with India. Before independence, inter-regional and inter-religious tensions became pronounced immediately after Jammu, Kashmir and Ladakh were welded into a single political entity with full backing from the colonial supremacy. As the Dogra rulers were fundamentally despotic, feudal and sectarian, the people of the State, particularly Muslims, got alienated and fought against the Dogra domination which culminated in the termination of Dogra Raj in 1947. However, till date the Dogras did not compromise with this, what they regarded humiliation to their collective pride. It is not therefore surprising that they harbour the dreams of carving out a separate state for Jammu and the anti-Kashmiri sentiment has become a fertile ground for 'conflict entrepreneurs' of Hindutva forces. But this sentiment is restricted among the Hindu populated areas of the Jammu province. In fact, they demand sub-regional autonomy to safeguard their political, cultural and economic interests from the monopolistic political tradition. Similarly in Kashmir, the political leaders both extremist and mainstream have totally failed to accommodate the minority aspirations of the other two regions and to form a single state. This led to the estrangement demands from the other two regions- Jammu and Ladakh. Since independence, the regional demands from Jammu were in the form of demand for abrogation of Article 370 and the slogan of "*Ek Desh Mai Do Pradhan, Do Vidhan, Do Nishan Nahi Chaleyga Nahi Chalega*" (in a single nation, the two presidents, two states and two symbols cannot be tolerated in any how). This voice has become louder again with the eruption of land controversy over the Amarnath land issue in Jammu, an agitation sponsored by Hindutva forces in August 2008. While in Kashmir, the Extremist groups took the stand and thus the two communities again got alienated. Last twenty years of political uncertainty in Jammu and Kashmir have created regional tensions at large. Of late, these tensions have created impressions that the state may soon fall apart. More painful is the fact that these differences have sharpened the communal divide. Amarnath land row in 2008 stands as an example of intolerance that the two main regions of Kashmir and Jammu have imbibed over a period. This divide was not only confined to these regions but has taken over the whole politics of the state up to the district level.

It is true that some rulers from the Kashmir region in the past have not acted according to the needs and aspirations of some of the people of Jammu and Ladakh. However, it is also true that Jammu and Ladakh regions always have had New Delhi's political and administrative favours on their side. New Delhi's such proximity and special favour to Jammu and Ladakh have bred feelings of psychological and political siege among Kashmir's civil society and political leadership. This feeling is reinforced with each passing day. Whenever there is a movement against Kashmir, the agitator would often allege that people of both Jammu and Ladakh regions do not receive any fair and equitable treatment. They insist that the government should ensure a sense of equality among the people of three regions and the existing regional identities should be maintained and kept intact. Therefore, the entire fabric of politics in the state has been mainly based on two issues; the relationship between the Kashmir valley and the centre on the one hand and the relationship between the Kashmir valley, Jammu and Ladakh regions within on the other. As Hari Om says, "A sort of local nationalism had developed in all the three regions of the state".

The unsettled nature of the political status of Jammu and Kashmir is a reality. The massive exploitation of its resources by New Delhi and to some extent by Islamabad has enlarged the debate on political justice in the state. However, the discourse on regional, sub-regional and ethnic identities is a new construct that has served two purposes. First, it has created a 'complex' issue out of a simple issue of self-determination of this former princely state. Secondly, it has sought to create an aggressor out of the victim- the Muslims of the J&K state. The result is tragic, as today almost all the communities in the state are up in arms against each other-making use of regional, sub-regional and ethnic identity cards to promote their economic interests.

The political divergence has often become the basis of politicisation by the political groups and organisations situated in the three regions of the state. Right from the time of state's accession in 1947, politics has been generated around the issue of Jammu's regional interest vis-à-vis Kashmir. The political discourse of regional discrimination and political deprivations claiming themselves has popularised the movements either for trifurcation of the state or for the demand for Regional Autonomy among these three regions. Also, political divergence at the inter-regional level that makes the process of peace and regional integration more challenging, especially at the internal level between the Government of India and the separatists of Kashmir. The local sensitivities in this context assume importance because the issue of political divergence between Jammu and Kashmir is highly compatible to the peace process, initiated by the Government of India, takes cognizance of the need to involve the political leadership that claims to represent the people of the three regions. Because it is always the aggressive political articulations of regional politics during the last one and half decades resulted in the demand that the process of conflict resolution should be both inclusive and participatory - inclusive enough to provide an opportunity to the regional leadership to negotiate the regional interest.

However, the complexity of the issue of peace, dialogue and regional integration is provided not as much by the multiplicity of political voices as by their divergence from the Ladakh Buddhist Association, Bhartiya Janta Party, Jammu Mukti Morcha, Jammu State Morcha, Panun Kashmir and Separatist Leadership in Kashmir etc. In context of political divergence, the idea of an intra-state dialogue has acquired prominence. The demand for an intra-state dialogue has not been raised only by the Jammu based political leaders who fear marginalisation of their voices in the peace process but also by the Kashmiri separatists who concede the possibility of failure of the process in the absence of an internal synchronisation of political views. Abdul Gani Lone, the leader of the People's Conference, was among the first separatist leaders who recognised the need to engage the voices outside the separatist politics to evolve a broad-based consensus towards the resolution of Kashmir problem. He had organised the first such meeting in Jammu where leaders across the political spectrum were invited to voice their opinion on the issue. Most of the Regional Autonomy politics were operating in terms of "we" and "they". It has been constructed around the polarity between different regions and sub-regions. It is not only the politics of "Jammu versus Kashmir" or "Kashmir versus Ladakh" that has been sharpened in the last few years, but also the politics of "Leh versus Kargil", "Jammu versus Doda" and "Jammu versus Poonch – Rajouri" etc.

The internal polarisation that has taken place, consequently has dangerous potential as it can provide substance to divisive agendas. Like, the people of Jammu and Ladakh have traditionally adopted a negative attitude over the special status of the state; the two regions have never supported the special status of the state under Article 370 of Indian constitution. Instead of this they have been demanding its abrogation. However, living in present status of affairs these two regions have been demanding devolution of more powers under the state constitution. The state is heterogeneous in character but has been placed under a unitary cost. This has hindered the flow of powers to all the regions of the state because of domination of Kashmiri leaders. Beyond the Valley of Kashmir, the demand for 'greater autonomy' has evoked emotions of different kind after the demand for resolution by State Autonomy Committee in June 2000. In the regions of Jammu and Ladakh, there has been strong opposition to the pre-1953 stance of the report of the State Autonomy Committee. The strong wave of resentment against the report has been a result of the Kashmir centric approach of the report that not only ignores the plural realities of the state but also undermines the regional aspirations. It is felt that autonomy for the state may actually come to mean autonomy for Kashmir only. It may not flow to the regional and sub-regional levels. The indifference on the part of the State Government on the demand for devolution of power becomes clear from the fact that there has been no Panchayat election in this state in last 22 years. The state has still to bring its Panchayat Raj Acts of 1989 at par with the 73rd Amendment Act of the constitution of India. To overcome such diverse tendencies it becomes important to build bridges between the regions and sub-regions through the process of dialogue. Also, in order to avoid tensions within the state, number of formulas have been floated from time to time – like the *Regional Autonomy Formula* by National Conference, *The Self Rule Proposal* by Peoples Democratic Party, *The Chenab Formula*, *Ladakh Autonomous Hill Council Model,* besides the internal demands of organisations like Jammu State Morcha and Ladakh Buddhist Association to reorganise the state by separating Jammu and Ladakh from Kashmir. But these formulas do not match with the ground realties and are not with harmony to the long-established socio-cultural identity aspirations of the region. That is why these formulas are not being taken very seriously at the local level.

Therefore, the regional analysis of the popular political aspirations of the people of Jammu and Kashmir State is based on the "cause and effect" relationship. There is no consensus among the people living in different regions of the state with respect to their political future. They stand divided along the regional, religious and ethnic lines. Considering the physical and social diversity of the state, its spatial and cultural ties with its neighbouring countries, any effort to make Jammu and Kashmir either an independent country or a part of Pakistan or a part of India will not be acceptable to the people of the state entirely. It is a fact that everybody talks about the unity of state but in practice divisions are so deep that even the people from regions didn't want to see eye to eye. For example, the intra-regional divisions within Jammu are deepening with each passing day. Demand of Chenab Valley Hill Development Council for Doda region and Pir Panjal Hill Development Council for Poonch-Rajouri is gaining momentum. In the former case, State Legislative Council has recently passed a resolution for the same. Similarly, the demand for Pir Panjal Council is being supported by most of the politicians and civil society members from the region. Their argument is very simple, "we have suffered at the hands of Jammu from last sixty three years." Going by the figures, their representation in employment and policy-making is negligible and that is why they push for an arrangement akin to the Hill Development Councils in Leh and Kargil. Therefore, the study suggests that, in order to find a permanent solution to the Kashmir problem in general and regional tensions in particular, the people of all regions need to be consulted by both the countries to ascertain their regional aspirations. Equitable empowerment is an alternative to both the divisions of Jammu and Kashmir. This simple formula will be to bring the people closer to each other and ensure unity; otherwise, no power can restrain the disgruntled sufficiently from pursuing the agenda of divisions and further divisions of the state. Looking at the deep divisions and prejudice, Jammu and Kashmir State today stands at the crossroads. One way from here goes to absolute anarchy and eventual divorce between Jammu, Kashmir and Ladakh. Another way leads to honest introspection and reconciliation. The first responsibility towards reconciliation lies at New Delhi's doorsteps to reverse all the policies which have served to breed divisions in the state. The second responsibility lies with the State Government to promote inter-regional understanding. The government policies which serve the island mentality in the three regions have to be abandoned. The study also suggests that the government must bring out a white paper on the real state of empowerment and disempowerment in the three regions. It has to come up with real statistics, whatever they are. There should be educational, cultural and political exchanges between the three regions, mainly among the youth. There should be debates surrounding a perfect vision of a common future. At a different level, the recruitment boards have to be reconstructed. The way the recruitment boards are constituted in favour of one particular region is preposterous.

Recruitment to government services, most importantly to Indian and Kashmir Administrative Services, must factor in proportions. They must be free and fair. More importantly, the study further reveals that the people of the state need to be allowed to have inter-ethnic, inter-religious and inter-regional dialogue to develop consensus to fulfil the mutually antagonistic political aspirations of the people living in different regions of the state. The state needs a multi-layered package of autonomy that must extend beyond the state to the regional and sub-regional levels. The unitary character of the Constitution of the state needs to be amended to adopt regional devolution of powers so that the divergent regional pulls and pushes of three regions of the state can be addressed. Until all these regions, especially Jammu and Kashmir join hands and set to work together, the regional tensions would continue to mar their relations. Hence, the need is to develop a democratic, federal, plural and non-centralised type of model that alone can ensure harmony among diverse identities of the state and make them a source of real strength and model for other states of India.

Bibliography

Primary Sources

- *A Hand Book of Jammu and Kashmir.*
- *Election Manifesto in 2008, Jammu and Kashmir Peoples Democratic Party.*
- *Flames of Chinar, Sheikh Mohammad Abdullah: An Autobiography.*
- *Human Development Report forward 1995.*
- *Ladakh Autonomous Hill Development Council Act. Govt. of Jammu and Kashmir,* May 1995.
- *Naya Kashmir published by secretary, All Jammu and Kashmir National Conference* 1944.
- *Puri, Balraj, Jammu and Kashmir Regional Autonomy: A Report, Jay Kay* Publishing House, Jammu.
- *Report of Regional Autonomy Committee, government of Jammu and Kashmir,* April 1999.
- *Report, Jammu and Kashmir Commission of Enquiry, Dec 1968.*
- *Self-Rule Document of Jammu and Kashmir Peoples Democratic Party,* Srinagar, 2008.
- *State Autonomy Committee Report Government of Jammu and Kashmir, 2000.*
- *The Jammu and Kashmir Assembly Debates.*
- *The Sikri Commission report and Regional Imbalances in Jammu and Kashmir,* Srinagar. 1982.
- *White Paper on Indian States; Government of India, Ministry of States,* New Delhi, 1950.
- *White paper on Jammu and Kashmir 1948.*

Secondary Sources/Books and Articles

- Akbar, M. J. *Kashmir Behind the Vale*, Roti Books Pvt. Ltd., New Delhi, 2000.
- Anand Justice, A. S. *The Constitution of J&K: Its Development and comment*, Delhi Universal Book Traders, edition 2004.
- B. Forrester Duncan, *Sub-regionalism in India*, Pacific Affairs, Spring, 1970.
- Bamzai, P. N. K. *History of Kashmir*, A Metropolitan Book Co. Pvt., New Delhi, 1962.
- Basu, D. D. *Introduction to the Constitution of India,* 19th edition 2007, Wadhwa and Company law publishers, New Delhi.
- Basu, Sajal, *Regional Movements: Politics of language, ethnicity and identity*, Indian Institute of Advance Study, Simla, 1992.
- Bazaz, P.N. *Kashmir in Crucible*, Pamposh Publication, New Delhi, 1967.
- Behera, N. C. *State Identity and Violence, Jammu and Kashmir*, Manohar Pub., Delhi, 1999.
- Behera Navnita C. *Demystifying Kashmir*, Pub. Dorling Kindersley (India), Delhi, 2007.
- Bhushan, Vidhaya, *Jammu and Kashmir Politics: Its Critical Aspects*, Yak publishing channel, Jammu, 2008.
- Bose, Sumantra, *Roots of conflict and paths to peace*, Vistar publications, New Delhi, 2003.
- Bose, Sumantra, *The challenge in Kashmir: Democracy, Self Determination and a just Peace*, Sage Publications, New Delhi, 1997.
- Brass Paul, R. *The Politics of India Since Independence, 2nd edition*, Cambridge University Press, 1990,
- Chattopadhyay, *Ethnic Composition and Crisis in South Asia*, Global vision Pub., Delhi, 2003.
- Chowdhary, Rekha, (ed.), *Identity Politics in Jammu and Kashmir*, Vitasta Publications, New Delhi, 2010.

- Fazli Manzoor, *Kashmir Govt. and Politics*, Gulshan Publishers, Srinagar, 1988.
- Fazli Manzoor, *Kashmir Predilection* (ed.), Gulshan Publishers, Srinagar, 1988.
- Ganguly, Sumit, *The Kashmir Question retrospect and prospect*, Frank CASS, Great Britan, 2003.
- Ghai, Yash, *Ethnicity and Autonomy: A framework for Analysis, in autonomy and ethnicity*, Ghai (ed.), Pub. Cambridge University Pres.
- Habibullah Wajahat, *My Kashmir Conflict and the prospects of enduring peace*, United States Institute of Peace, 2008.
- Haward B. Schaffer, *The limits of influence; America's role in Kashmir*, Brookings Institute Press 2009.
- Hedwig Hintze, *Encyclopedia of Social Sciences*, Vol. XII-XIV, New York, Macmillan, 1924, pp. 208-218.
- Hindutva Shakti Kak. *The Crisis of the state and political mobilisation in Jammu and Kashmir,* Contemporary perspectives of History and Sociology, Vol. 3, No. 1, Jan – June 2009, Cambridge University Press – India Pvt. Ltd.
- Iffat Malik, *Kashmir ethnic conflict, international dispute*, Oxford University Press, 2005.
- Iqbal Narrain, *Regional Politics in India* in P. C. Mathur (ed.), *Govt. and Politics in South Asia*, Printwell Pub. Jaipur, 1985.
- Iyer, R. R. Indus Treaty: *A Different View*, Economic and Political Weekly, Vol. 11, n. 29 (16 July 2005).
- Iyon Peter, *Conflict between India and Pakistan; an encyclopedia*, ABC –CLIO, 2008.
- Jina, Prem Singh, *Ladakh: Past and Present*, Gyan Publishing House, New Delhi, 2002.
- *Journal on Peace initiatives; Next steps in Jammu and Kashmir*, Give peace a chance, Vol. vi, Nos. iv-vi, July-December, 2000.
- K Nayar, V. *Crossing the Frontiers of Conflict*, Shipra Publisher New Delhi.

- K. Majumdar A. and Bhanwar Singh, (eds.) *Regionalism in Indian Politics*, Radha Publications, New Delhi, 1997.
- Kak, B. L. *Chasing Shadows in Ladakh*, Light and Life Publishers, New Delhi, 1978.
- Kapoor, M. L. *History of Jammu and Kashmir, The Making of the State*, Gulshan Books Publications, Srinagar, 2005.
- Kaul, B. L. *Kashmir: Problem and politics*, Seema Publications New Delhi, 1981.
- Kaul, G. L. *Kashmir through Ages,* Chronicle Publishing House, Srinagar, 1967.
- Kaul, Santosh, *Freedom struggle in Jammu and Kashmir*, Anmol Publications, New Delhi, 1990.
- Kaul, Pyarelal, *Kashmir Crisis*, Suman Pub., Srinagar, 1999.
- Kaul, Shyan and Onkar Kachru, *Jammu, Kashmir and Ladakh: Ringside Views,* Atlantic Publications, New Delhi, 1998.
- Kaul, Sridhar and H. Kaul, *Ladakh through the Ages: towards a new identity*, Indus Publishing Company, New Delhi, 1992.
- Kaur, Ravinderjit, *Political awakening in Kashmir*, Ashish Publications, New Delhi, 1996.
- Kaur, Ravinderjit, *Why Autonomy to Kashmir,* Institute of Peace and Conflict studies, September 2003.
- Khan, G. H. *Government and politics of Jammu and Kashmir*, Light and Life Publications, Jammu.
- Khan, G.H. *Freedom in Kashmir 1931- 1940*, Light and Life Publications, New Delhi, 1980.
- Khatana, R. R. *Educational Neglect of Gujjar Community: Awaze-e-Gujjar*, June-July 1996.
- Khatana, R.P. *Gujri Language and Identity in Jammu and Kashmir*; *Awaz-e-Gujjar,* January 1996.
- Kishtwari, Aseer, *Focus on Jammu and Kashmir*, Crescent Publications, Jammu, 2006.
- Kumar, Ashutosh, *Some thoughts on the debate on Autonomy in Jammu and Kashmir*, Mainstream, December 23, 2000.

- Lamb, Alaster, *Kashmir: A Disputed Legacy 1846-1990*, Oxford University Press, 1991.
- Lapidoth Ruth, *Autonomy, Flexible Solutions to ethnic Conflicts*, (Washington, D.C; United States Institute of Peace, 1996).
- Lawrence Walter, *The Valley of Kashmir*, Oxford University Press, 1895.
- Magray, Bashir, *Tribal geography of India – Jammu and Kashmir*, Oberio Book Service, Jammu, 2003.
- Malik Hafeez, *US relations with Afghanistan and Pakistan*, the imperial Oxford University Press, 2008,
- Mandla, Sunita, *Politics of State autonomy and regional identity in J&K*, Delhi, Kalpaz Publications, 2006.
- Narrain, Iqbal, *Cultural Pluralism, National Integration and Democracy in India*, Asian survey, XVI October 10, 1976.
- Om, Hari and Rekha Chowdhery, (ed.) *Politics of Autonomy*, Vinod Publishers, Jammu, 1999.
- Om, Hari, *Special Status in Indian Federation Jammu and Kashmir*, Seema Publication, Delhi, 1983.
- P. Kumar, *Kashmir Return to Democracy*, Cosmo Publications, India, 1996.
- P.N. Bazaz, *The History of Struggle for freedom*, Kashmir Publishing House, New Delhi, 1955.
- Pampori, M. S. *Kashmir in chains, 1819-1992,* Pampori Publishing House, Srinagar.
- Pandit, M. L. and T. N. Pundit, *Kashmiri Pundits: A contemporary perspective*, APH Publishing Corporations, New Delhi, 2005.
- Paul, T. V. *The India-Pakistan conflict an Enduring Rivalry* (edited), Cambridge University Press, 2005.
- Peter Lyon, *Conflict between India and Pakistan*: An Encyclopedia, ABC Publications, California, 2008.
- Punjabi, Riyaz, *Kashmiriyat: The Mystique of an Identity*, IIC Quarterly, New Delhi, Spring 1991.

- Puri, Balraj, *Identities, Ideologies and Politics in Jammu and Kashmir State*, The Journal of Kashmir Studies Centre, University of Kashmir, Hazratbal, Srinagar, 2006, Vol. 1.
- Puri, Balraj, *Jammu and Kashmir- An old solution*, the Daily Tribune, June 29, 1977.
- Puri, Balraj, *Jammu and Kashmir- Trumph and Tragedy of Indian Federalisation*, Sterling Publishers Pvt. Ltd., 1981.
- Puri, Balraj, *Jammu: A Clue to Kashmir Tangle, 1966.*
- Puri, Balraj, *Kashmir: Towards Insurgency*, Orient Longman Limited, New Delhi, 1995.
- Puri, Balraj, *Simmering Volcano – study of Jammu's Relations with Kashmir*, Sterling Publishers Pvt. Ltd, New Delhi, 1983.
- Puri Balraj, *Sub- Nationalism, Identities and National Integration,* Economic and Political Weekly Magazine, June 1976.
- R. Sharma Y. *Political Dynamics of Jammu and Kashmir*, Publisher Anand Radhakrishan, Jammu, 2002.
- Rafique Anjum, *Evolution of Gujri Language*: *Awa-e- Gujjar*, January 1996.
- Rai, Mridu, *Hindu Rulers and Muslim Subjects*, Permanent Black Publisher, Delhi, 2004.
- Reddy, B. Muralidhar, *The Mushraf Formula, Frontline,* Vol. 21. Issue 23 Nov. 06-19- 2004.
- Reddy, G.R. and Sharma, B.K. *Regionalism in India,* Concept Publishing Company, New Delhi, 1979.
- S. Verma, P. *Jammu and Kashmir politics*, in the Indian Journal of Political Science, Vol. VVVI, no. 7, March – Sep. 1987.
- Samaddar, Ranabir, (ed.) *The Politics of Autonomy – Indian Experience*, Sage Publication, New Delhi, 2005.
- Saraf, Pushp. *Border Affairs*, Vol. 3, April – June 2008.
- Saxena, Ashish, *Reflections on Democratic Decentralisation in Jammu and Kashmir*, Economic and Political Weekly Magazine, March 1, 2008.
- Schofield, Victoria, *Kashmir in Conflict, India, Pakistan and the unending war*, Viva Books, New Delhi, 2004.

- Shah, Farzana, *Chenab Formula*, Pakistan Times, Tuesday September 23, 2008.
- Sharma, Daya Sagar, *PDP has intelligent game plan; appears training the decade's old NC roadmap,* American Chronicle, Kashmir Affairs, September 8, 2009.
- Shri Prakash and Shah, G. M. (eds.), *Towards understanding the Kashmir Crisis*, Gyan Publishing House, New Delhi, 2002.
- Singh, M.P. and Mohan Chandra (eds.), *Regionalism and Nation Identity Canadian and Indian Perspective,* Pragati pub., Delhi, 1994.
- Sinha Aditya, *Farooq Abdullah Kashmir's Prodigal Son: A Biography*, UBS Publishers, New Delhi, 1995.
- Spalbar, Rigzin, *Why Union Territory for Ladakh*, *Epilogue Magazine*, February 2010, Vol. 14, Issue 2.
- Swami, Praveen, *India, Pakistan and the secret jihad, the covert war in Kashmir, 1947-2004*, Routledge Taylor and Francis group, New York, 2007.
- Teng M. K. *State Govt. and Politics, Jammu and Kashmir*, Sterling Publisher, New Delhi.
- Thomas, Bonedikter, *Territorial Autonomy: A Solution for open Ethnic Conflicts*, Foreign Affairs (March 20, 2008).
- Thomas, R.G.C. (ed.) *Perspectives on Kashmir: The roots of conflict in south Asia*, Boulder Colo, West View Press, 1992.
- Timothy D. Sisk, *Power sharing and international mediation in ethnic conflicts,* United States Institute of Peace (Washington, D.C; 1996).
- U. K. Zutshi, *Emergence of political awakening in Kashmir*, Manhor Publications, New Delhi, 1986.
- Varshey, Ashutosh, *India, Pakistan and Kashmir- Antinomies of Nationalism*, in Asian Survey, Vol. XXXXI, No. 11, Nov. 1991.
- Verma, P.S. *Jammu and Kashmir at the Political Cross Roads,* New Delhi, 1994.
- Verma, R K. *Regionalism and sub-regionalism in state politics social, economic, and political bases,* Deep Publisher Delhi, 1994.

- Waslekar, S. *The Final Settlement: Restructuring India-Pakistan Relations* (Mumbai: Strategic Foresight Group, 2005).
- Wirsing, Robert G. India, *Pakistan and the Kashmir Dispute on Regional Conflicts and its Resolution*, St. Martin's Press, New York, 1994.
- Wirsing, Robert G. *Kashmir in the shadows of war, Regional Rivalries in a Nuclear Age*, Pub. M.E. Sharpe, New York, 2002.

Interviews

- Ab. GaniVakil
- Balraj Puri
- Dr. Farooq Abdullah
- Naeem Akther
- Prof. Rekha Chowdhary
- Prof. Sidiq Wahid

Journals, Magazines Local/National

- Conveyor, Jammu and Kashmir
- Economic and Political Weekly, New Delhi
- Epilogue, Jammu and Kashmir
- Frontline, Chennai
- Frontline, New Delhi
- Indian Journal of Politics (Quarterly)
- Kashmir Scan, Jammu and Kashmir
- Kashmir Speaks, Jammu and Kashmir
- Mainstream, New Delhi
- South Asian Survey
- The Honour, Jammu and Kashmir

National News Papers

- The Hindu, Chennai
- The Hindustan Times, New Delhi
- The Indian Express, Chandigarh
- The Statesman
- The Times of India, New Delhi

Local News Paper

- Aftab (Urdu), Srinagar
- Chatan (Weakly), Srinagar
- Daily Excelsior, Jammu
- Kashmir life (Weekly News Paper)
- Kashmir Times, Srinagar
- Kashmir Uzma (Urdu), Srinagar
- Rising Kashmir, Srinagar
- Srinagar Times (Urdu), Srinagar
- The Etalaat (Urdu), Srinagar
- The Greater Kashmir, Srinagar
- The Kashmir Images, Srinagar

Index

C

R

S